Society Awaken
BOOK 1

Society doesn't include disability fairly

Jd. Rodriguez

ISBN 978-93-5458-406-0
© Jd. Rodriguez 2021
Published in India 2021 by Pencil

A brand of
One Point Six Technologies Pvt. Ltd.
123, Building J2, Shram Seva Premises,
Wadala Truck Terminal, Wadala (E)
Mumbai 400037, Maharashtra, INDIA
E connect@thepencilapp.com
W www.thepencilapp.com

DISCLAIMER: *The opinions expressed in this book are those of the authors and do not purport to reflect the views of the Publisher.*

Author biography

Fairytale childhood all changed, a tough life led him off the rails. He drank in consolidation but carried on when he began driving.

He crashed his car, he had not witnessed struggle until the onset of disability. He was to relearn everything from his own mind to what society had to offer. A new realm of existence that naivity did not prepare him for.

Lost all his so called mates, fell out with family lots and became very isolated. So getting back into writing he records pretty much most his life, as he has had a lot of life taught lessons and coming from a background as a speaker he journals everything anti-drink-driving to educate.

He utilizes his disability and the stories invoked by an all understanding society to deter the idiots game. Is family was told in the very early days he may never walk or talk again, he worked hard at his rehabilitation and proved professionals wrong at every junction, now look at him.

CONTENTS

Whole book

Apology.

I want to reasure you all, I claim no innocence when it comes to this. We all discriminate without even realizing sometimes.

I said in an earlier publishes that you want to stay in fitness, or find trouble with doing absolutely everything, disabled people, and here is what I could have said, can have trouble doing the smallest thing. When I said you will get satisfaction from doing the most mundane, I did not intend all disabled people do, I was referring to myself and others after brain-injury.

Some disabled people absolutely carry life like anyone else, saying that they have to remain very strong characters.

I think this is why there is still such a massive difficulty campaigning and making a difference because I suspect other campaigners like myself and the genera- public do not even realize they are doing anything wrong and when this is so often brought up as a topic by disabled people, so often why we get a reputation for always moaning. The majority of people cannot comprehend or sense these issues as very minor, but you have heard the saying start small think big, however this goes, well even the tiniest changes can have big impact The tiny occurance happening ten times or more per day can determine a big influence on the sufferer.

I apologize profusely and promise to only publish more works on cream paper. I tried changing the settings to go to cream paper but this said cannot change after publish. I was saving money as my early work was done on a budget.

1- Boredom mounts advantage takers take - vulnerability and isolation.
2- Disability and drink - assumptions from a 'knowing' society.
3- Dont do this dont do that - Discrimination secrets revealed.
4- Emotions rule - experiments, self driving cars. ethics, emotions, disability acceptance.
5- establish sense - Avoidance.
6- Facades deduce - Good intention, jealousy, false fronts, ignorance, childhood.
7- Follow your purpose - Differing forms of people.
8- Memories from my past - Is this really mental health?
9- Mum- Brief my story.
10- Psychology - Realities, beliefs, Zen.
11- The mystical - Spirituality and deceit, because I thought.
12- Still have a brain - Lost my mind in rehab!
13- Summer - Crazy days, early awareness in hospital.
14- Susan - Unintended judgements, companionship, judgement, a death.
15- The door is wide - A new inception of disability exclusion and inclusion.
16- Intention; - A best society
17- Dont die a fool. The lessons are long and difficult or

sudden and devastating.

18- An abrupt end, dont die a fool

Fiction-reality. Did he die in the crash? ...or was that rehab?

He started life in a fairytale, then upheaval one after the other slowly degraded this. Then the absolute switch, which materialized over years. Now he recognizes faces from past, with story aligned, his thought dictate things are strange.

He walked the sublime now in matrimony. Reality is his for the making because past action has determined a world.

Neuro-rehab made him all better then swiped his livlyhood.

He calls Mum and asked if he was dead, this reality confuses.

So much manipulable so much adhered to and the enforced.

Oh thoughts get listened to, do they so and acted on, well why not my actions considering that is what humans are taught, most of humanity anyway, except for those exceptionally lucky minority that had parenting in the know.

I was taught this does not matter what ya think, ya cannot control your thought, this all depends on what action ya take.

I do not mean to talk in slang but this is all enveloped from spiritual emphasis having influence.

Because they thought, they chose and because this was wrong my life suffers. Because they fear they have done wrong, they affect my thought, my life to detriments that expose. They take so I expose.

They did this to a fine brain then listened to all the thought produced by an inhibited brain, I no longer have a mind, you find our why in my other books, all I say here this was enabled by them.

My totally abstract thought came to light and now all people are the same, minus the minority lucky few billion who are my neighbours and soon to become friends. Ya have a human feeling sorry for the awakened, yeah residing in human only category of existence. Missing the true deed am I? You're missing the true picture of my time.

Why affect others to inform when just leads to paranoia, mistaken ordeals and the rest. Yeah so I did not complete every demand, what goes for me goes for every awakened person, why no? That said I am refused by yourselves, that is right not fully awakened so I am exempt from this consideration.

Why give me power beyond your control or at least choice, if ya knew how things would go? But oh, ya suddenly have choice when this goes how ya not like, well I do not like either and this was all instigated by yourselves!

Synchronicities are a outweighed area, what is the reason? Because my overwhelmed brain said so, well if I can own that power, you are taking nothing from me and I promote all and every productive word I ever spoke and thought. Think ya can break rules just because ya made them, what goes for one goes for all, I remake and write my own productions.

I make my life, my protection what I always knew this would be. I am the god of my life, me not mistake thought or impeded upheaval.

Fiction-reality. Did he die in the crash? ...or was that rehab?

He started life in a fairytale, then upheaval one after the other slowly degraded this. Then the absolute switch, which materialized over years. Now he recognizes faces from past, with story aligned, his thought dictate things are strange.

He walked the sublime now in matrimony. Reality is his for the making because past action has determined a world.

Neuro-rehab made him all better then swiped his livlyhood.

He calls Mum and asked if he was dead, this reality confuses.

So much manipulable so much adhered to and the enforced.

Oh thoughts get listened to, do they so and acted on, well why not my actions considering that is what humans are taught, most of humanity anyway, except for those exceptionally lucky minority that had parenting in the know.

I was taught this does not matter what ya think, ya cannot control your thought, this all depends on what action ya take.

I do not mean to talk in slang but this is all enveloped from spiritual emphasis having influence.

Because they thought, they chose and because this was wrong my life suffers. Because they fear they have done wrong, they affect my thought, my life to detriments that expose. They take so I expose.

They did this to a fine brain then listened to all the thought produced by an inhibited brain, I no longer have a mind, you find our why in my other books, all I say here this was enabled by them.

My totally abstract thought came to light and now all people are the same, minus the minority lucky few billion who are my neighbours and soon to become friends. Ya have a human feeling sorry for the awakened, yeah residing in human only category of existence. Missing the true deed am I? You're missing the true picture of my time.

Why affect others to inform when just leads to paranoia, mistaken ordeals and the rest. Yeah so I did not complete every demand, what goes for me goes for every awakened person, why no? That said I am refused by yourselves, that is right not fully awakened so I am exempt from this consideration.

Why give me power beyond your control or at least choice, if ya knew how things would go? But oh, ya suddenly have choice when this goes how ya not like, well I do not like either and this was all instigated by yourselves!

Synchronicities are a outweighed area, what is the reason? Because my overwhelmed brain said so, well if I can own that power, you are taking nothing from me and I promote all and every productive word I ever spoke and thought. Think ya can break rules just because ya made them, what goes for one goes for all, I remake and write my own productions.

I make my life, my protection what I always knew this would be. I am the god of my life, me not mistaken thought or impeded upheaval.

Disability. Well fair. NOT.

He had been severely disabled years back. Some people think a physical disability is ever endured or he was born that way. He made massive improvements both physically and cognitively with long rehabilitation. The epiphany of such healing along with other tremendously affecting facets left him with accepted mental health issues. These however were not accepted by him, other entities caused him difficulty added to the norm of people not broaching the subject in mind, he distilled to categorize this agenda minutely and go with the masses. In one-to-one speech anyway but he agrees he has yielded to this law while writing. His freedom of speech is not held back in the written word, sometimes over the top different proposals intend him to find difficulty in locating the horizon. Some say this is filled with wealth of all nature and joy while others predict quite the opposite.

Amid a taken for granted and fully accepted assumption of mental health problems this adds to anxieties. He however is strong, more so than he contemplates, which is taken and explained by some care providers, professionals, acquaintances, family and friends as only expected disillusionment.

He has changed past conditioning, as well as he can mus ta and stays on a chosen path. He kept referring to, throughout his previous books, disability equality. Not because he considers himself in a challenging situation but because of his past, before rehabilitation and years of recovery and adjustments, he knows like other disabled people do just what we face when fronted with a comprehending society, humanity is not so humane. The barriers, social and physical can crush the sense of self.

A lot assume disability is something to be pitied, and will

not pick up on a condescending tone. Oh you are doing so well, keep going, you are so brave after what you have been through, keep this up. Coming from an absolute stranger in the street is condescending and patronizing.

People are all categorized differently through their own making. You still get the nice well-wishers, even so they are often disregarded a little because we are just going about our daily business and do not need reminding of what we have been through or what struggles we have or the obstructions or the negative categorization. He admits to similar category making through no choice in the becoming thin on the ground possible companions.

So he has a new mission set, while trying to remain unfazed by all this and that is to write about disability. He has a bad limp and is weak down one side but like this was spoken of, he remembers the very much impeding years of disabled life and wishes to promote change and education is the way forward.

We all desire equal citizenship, Morris (2005) believes in terms of disability that citizenship arrives in three forms; self-determination, participation and contribution.

There are arguments for each and I base these largely on social-attitudes and education. Society attempts to determine a lack of self-belief in the seen as needy and incapable.

Participation contribution both have there barriers, we are often automatically excluded from consideration of these and attempts at either are frequently looked at as look at the disabled one trying to find something to do and fit in or they are trying to feel of some importance in the world, bless.

Separation from the mainstream society partly he thinks

goes unappreciated and just an automatic assumption. Every one has their qualities, different people are better at some things than others who are even better at a different subject. He can write and he knows people who are dyslexic who have admirable qualities beyond his scope. We accept differing attitudes in people as no one the same, why not abilities? Most people when asked totally believe they do not discriminate, talking in a slow or loud tone because someone thinks or walks differently is a form

of discrimination. Believe me or not, waiting for or offering an exaggerated time or needless assistance for the simple tasks easily carried out is discrimination while many consider this necessary and that they are acting as an important contribution to society. He can tell by the facial expressions what makes people feel good and what amuses them. He is more astute than many in less regarded things, things he knows bring enormous value to his existence yet still slow on the uptake sometimes in taken for granted areas. This all makes a task out of feeling just a sense of belonging. Enough of anything can cause a self-for filling prophecy in all people, so people with disabilities always under the impression that they are a nuisance or scrounging or needy or to feel pity for may eventually likely bear down and unconsciously affect demeanour or even the physical body, fact! Can you believe? This is the science of the human mind.

Disabled people are amongst the most creative, narrative people, genuinely most are nice by nature, influenced timidity causes a picture to get painted by the rest of society as disability is unapproachable or to be avoided. Talk down to a child and they will mature unconfidently, the oppression disabled people are against is the vastness of humanity with all their assumptions. Challenging attitudes is one of the largest invisible obstacles faced. An acknowledgement from all that impairments of all kinds are a natural part of getting older.

Sociologists and scientists researched disability since the 50s (Barnes 2014), much went unwarranted because they approached this by taking a medical model. That holds the view that disadvantaged people is caused by the direct outcome of disability, when the social model and societal walls were not taken into consideration. Social influence can be a true cause of people getting regarded as second class citizens and affects more than the impairment. Rather than suggestive saying that disabled people are somehow broken the model that agrees with societal influence senses the necessity for alterations in the environment.

He walked into a pub and was refused to get served because he was assumed drunk, people on the street often look disgusted at him for getting so drunk in the morning when this was his usual walking style.

He approached the doors to nightclubs and blatantly refused entry by bouncers because he was thought drunk. He recalls this on many incidents in every town, now he refuses to go clubbing, lucky he can just about get heard shouting over the music but this was a struggle to manoeuvre in a bustling club. Tired of the stigma shown by staff and public, the self for filling prophecy hatched and today he does not feel free to go in busy places, even be a house guest at someone he does not know.

He was in a bar with some people he met in hospital, one sat swaying, one shouted random phrases and the other drooled and had to be fed his drink thickened through a straw. Normality for them but the whole bar had stopped their drinking conversations and was utterly awestruck! Disability a natural part of millions of lives can completely silence a room, onlookers gazing in disbelief as if at the cinema in front of a captivating film.

A friend in a wheelchair often gets spoken over or in a derogatory tone, just because he cannot walk does not imply stupidity.

Disabled people are conditioned to act and behave, even acquire a look of disability. No I am not talking rubbish, the sub-conscious will alter the brain plasticity even the physical body to comply with what is observed most. Yes a lot self-generated- by constantly saying thanks for menial assistance from an over bearing kindness some possess. I was at a house party years ago, we were drunk, I was freshly without mind and lost all inhibition. I approached a girl I had taken a liking to, because I recalled my ease in approaching females before the accident and the welcome response I often got. Still in tune to the emotions of others even after a drink and the rehab incident, I could sense the whole room was uncomfortable for a disabled person on a drunken prowl. Felt unease I muttered an intoxicated chat up.This was totally explainable to others, as what you expect from people like him and she immediately exited the room, not given chance when later I tried to apologize I was either utterly disregarded as a drunk fool or the disabled one to avoid. Passing people on the street years later that were at that party their dismissive demeanour told me this was the latter.

We get used to seclusion, isolation and lack of comprehension.

This really is an alternative reality, that cannot get believed until entrance, once here you suddenly appreciate all your prior mistakes, your health and the little things. Care workers good enough to work shorter hours on a bank holiday make all the difference to my part isolation. Your appreciation increases and you finally consider the really hard done by. Not just a whimsical patronising self-considered comprehension but a real feeling of compassion. Just like no-one will ever know what the thrill is of climbing the highest mountain or mining the deepest cave until they themselves have scoured the heights or delved the abyss. Trekking snow and ice or sweating the desert. Becoming disabled midlife is a difficulty only those with disabilities can fully apprehend. Stay in the easier side of life, you want everything to become a struggle meaning you gain satisfaction at the most mundane accomplishments.

Respect your fitness now, hold onto pleasant emotions, never drink/drug drive or speed.

Dread occurs from past experiences, things you witness including the things you are told. The more prominant a position someone is in the more you will retain and take as truth.

So when you witness in whatever form a terrible event, you now have that image ingrained, to get brought into consciousness when occurrence reminds of this event. You then may have some anxiety that the same thing will happen.

WELL, a Neuro-Psychologist predicted some terrible events I recall as I am reminded, NOW I have anxiety!

Look at my other books if you want the full story. I am going to talk about this here. This is why I have anger at him and all allowing entities.

I graduated rehab, destroyed at the end now years later

reality is not what I dreamed of. My past has included times of no fear, hate or hostility from myself. Though I did receive some hostility at times, I feel more of all three today than ever. All be it part self-induced, if you insist on remaining unnaware the unknown will succumb. I had mystical encounters that promised a fabulous future but denial in me has brought me here.

Am I over thinking? I feel like this addiction is little chosen but impeded on. When we start losing control we tend to overthink, parallesis is a strategy the famous survival instinct has. This vicious circle continues.

Doubt and imagination can be amongst the greatest of enemies, and visualization is the best treaty. We must learn to use our imagination not to dwell when focus is important like in an exam but to imagine the best outcome. Neurological pathways are not fixed, they are not connected as was the old belief. New findings show they merely point to each other, nothing is ever permanent you can create change, actually rewiring our minds. Bear this in mind next time you have a negative thought, part of my writing ambition is to work on myself but my calling will not let me forget purpose and helping others while I help myself is an all round win.

Emotional resilience a lot of us strive for. There are some very good free books I listen to online on mental toughness and emotional intelligence.

The work on myself is made difficult by my thoughts, I am trying to gain more control but that psychological impression and distant messages that I recall at the most inopportune moments have become habitually difficult to master. I am learning much as I am inspired to write for you all.

Listening to an audio that said the first philosophers did not ever have a big audience and their work only remains in small amounts. That got to me thinking about my audience and my deliverance and current confidence. I have a large audience but deliver through writing, I do not so much feel the empowerment to get up in front of people any more because at present I do not feel psychologically fit and memory, word finding, speaking does not accurately depict who I am and what I am capable of.

We must take the Stoic perspective and be ok with what happens by nature, even in confusing and uncertain times. I am ok with this in so much that I have found purpose in writing but am not settling for the past negative impressions that were made and left that keep cropping up and result in constant doubt. This is not suggested by any who have a clue, the more you think the more the universe and sub-conscious mind listen, and detailed in my other book, having affected ridiculous thought has been made accustommed to a once very agile mind.

Eudaimonia, how to be joyous and not let the small stuff be as bothersome, although my life has had joys it has also not so small occurrences. I need to focus on what I control.

Zeno 262BC, a famous Stoic would take his teaching out of a classroom and to the public where he could say controversial things to stimulate discussion and debate. I think he is a role model for the way I write. Look at my other book.

Even Zeno was not the perfect role model maybe, after suicide this does not promote the overall aims of Stoicism very well surely.

Reckless lives are rewarded, so is serenity, with like for like. 1- Boredom mounts advantage takers take - vulnerability and isolation.

A quiet experience can result in a person becoming more vulnerable, you will do anything for collaboration with peers, just conversation as your struggles with walking mean you do not go out much or you have spent all your money partly on entertaining the advantages and sure enough boredom sets in.

Trying to inspire yourself is made difficult with expectation of the serene except this serenity has murky skies. There is not much beauty in solitude, unless you are that way inclined, I am not this at all. Actually like everything this depends on how you view this time. Some will only love a quiet moment, radio on doing what they choose, these are mostly people with careers or other lifetime fillers, family, friends, business etcetera.

I choose to write, I am not one for chores or other entertainments, writing is a beautiful past time, the hours stream past and I get an adrenalin reward after writing a good piece. I feel I am of service because all my writing has a moral backing with reason. I talk a lot of my experiences but these have mainly only appeared because of my lack of sense. I was too content to plod on when most things were good so was shown, if I was not going to search for this extra to existence then I was to be shown another reality. One that I always felt immune from and denied appreciation of.

Do not take life or you ability for granted, you want to know why drunk driving and disability equality are such seriously taken topics? Or why mental health is somewhat a taboo issue, you can fully regard these from the place in the same direction as ignorance.

Your vulnerability will teach you much but in that position you have no stature to argue with a listened to voice. They say do not have regrets, this is very difficult when your own stupidity lands you in isolated matrimony. Look to the future is more advice, I am trying and only recently really envisage better things because there is some life style decisions on the horizon, but this is not possible when, as millions of people are entrapped in loneliness and isolation.

2- Disability and drink - assumptions from a 'knowing' society.

A wish to rectify the relationship between, and non judgemental acceptance, the able to the disabled. Talking to those who are not aware, do you realize how patronizing it is to refer to a disability first off and say 'your so strong, you've been through much' when they don't even know you, or to remark when someone in a wheelchair says I am just going to run to the shop. Common vocabulary is still used, everyday speech is hard to diverge but it seems this is shouting for listeners. An example of why your wrong if you do this exact example, my friend that had a severe disability, who joined an athletics club and was encouraged to, in a fashion jog, even attempt to jump small hurdles! So, you know the saying, judge, book, cover, don't.

Disability is not to be pitied, that is like pitying a child who stumbles, you just don't, you get them up, brush them off and give them some love and they are bouncing on their way.

These people are some of the most resilient people you

will meet but often we aren't given the time to get to know this. Disability faces obstacles the majority of you 'normal' folk won't even have nightmares about. True grit is required not to become isolated and venture into society. People think a commute to work can be stressful, how about thinking of every obstacle and all the barriers along with the looks from others, the kids remarks to Mum or Dad, not getting served in pubs because your assumed drunk, people going over roads because they dare not walk near the drunk or they are disillusioned by disability.

These people have a deeply seated fear, perhaps unconsciously because they sense a threat of they're own mortality, do not want 'that' in their own life so immediately don't relate. Or think that the disabled individual cannot master the simplest task, I have witnessed a blind man waiting for the beep at lights to go over a main road, on his own, no dog no stick, and another blind man, this time with a dog being extremely social in a pub enjoying himself. Now why can that not be comprehended by a majority?

Physical disability does not mean, because we look like we can't walk properly that we are stupid or can't manage. Take for granted some of us can and do, the rest of us have our own barriers to combat that is often taken as the cripple moaning but more likely totally out of your realm of appreciation.

I thought I was somewhat good at portraying my trials, my ego takes over when I consider myself as opposed to ignorance as an expert in minority ordeals, but I listened to an audio, Disability studies, by Colin Cameron. Their are people studying what I have been writing about in a less eloquent manner, and that have the articulacy to demonstrate efficiently. There are many experts out there, it makes little sense why disabled people are disregarded so much and even less sense why drink driving is still an issue. Thats what got me here, some people whether knowing or not sense the distaste of disability but will still drive drunk! The saying, the simplest things can reap the biggest rewards is the same as the easiest things can cause the most havoc. Drink driving is easy, easy done, are you easy? Do you want to be done? Done in?

My mother was getting out her car one day, she wobbled and stumbled a little, a passer gave her such a look of disgrace assuming she was drunk and getting out of a car had been drunk driving. Mum being as witty as she is just thought, go on say something and I will make you look this big. She did not say anything so Mum with her amazing temperance just kept quiet.

She has a Menieres disease which causes dizziness and effects her balance, that is all, she was not drinking. I commented it is good that you can have the confidence in a heated situation to have that intention and to not cause an uproar when things did not need words. A disabled person may not have this confidence or ability to remain calm and think of apt ways to effectively articulate, brain injury for example can cause word finding difficulties made worse when emotions rise.

 I am telling the stories of disability for a double purpose, to help all those drinkers really think about not driving, they can accept not wanting these words to include themselves and to improve acceptance and equal treatment for disabled people.

I have done this myself so know what struggle we have, I referred to non-disabled people as able, disabled are just as able in certain areas. This can be regarded as discrimination on my part, wholly unintentional but disabled people or activists may take offence to this speech. I comprehend what an uphill struggle disability equality is as myself has succumbed to some of the things I and others speak of. Discrimination can be unintended but just as harmful. I don't propose this intending total innocence.

When I spoke of language being misconstrued such as a disabled person running to the shop or I talk of or I hear you, there are many examples. I have mistakenly done this exact thing with a disabled friend whom is the final person I want to offend.

The stories of disability; Not much I will admit but I have done some research and the stories of disabled people were just like mine, hard to comprehend but true. This is happening so much and needs to stop. Mum listened to a very small part of an audio I bought about disability, she thought I had written it in part because she recognised so many of the 'tales' told. This is happening all about the world, the same or similar things, we need to believe when a story is repetitively told, disabled voices should be heard.

Memory can be recalled even though you may not recall the original justification, knowledge can be mistaken because of this. If information is delivered incorrectly you go about assuming this is true but your knowledge was wrong from the start.

3- Dont do this dont do that - Discrimination secrets revealed.

Don't do this, don't do that, drink driving is one discrimination is another. Just some out of the endless advice on do's and don't, so this is easily comprehensible that certain people choose to ignore advice or rules and practice the exact thing deterred. Comprehend this, that there are mystical essences influencing every area of our lives, so if you are secretly at something you should not, get real this is no secret and will have an affect in some form.

Dents or scratches on cars, this is where I started. Blissful I carried on, or possibly you are pulled over and breathalysed, perhaps you getaway with this, I did, blissful I carried on. Or perhaps you go to court, are sentenced, loose your license, your job, your livelihood, your social life and your respect. Or possibly, you have little choice if you are breaking the rules remember, these essences control much in your existence and you have a minor crash, this happened to me, blissful and pissed I carried on. Or quite likely you have a more serious crash, someone is hurt, so you loose all the above... and go to jail. Or just as likely, you cripple yourself, lose all the above, get charged some of the above, if you are well enough and have to start relearning simple life sequences, retraining your mind and skills, all is lost from the brain-damage. Perhaps you can walk, perhaps not, perhaps you can talk, perhaps not. Perhaps you wish you had died in the crash, theres nothing left to live for, perhaps you are strong and face your new life...

...Or quite probably, you smash your head open, sense your partner fly through the windscreen, then yourself die! Do we need to tempt fate? Do we need lessons? Do I need to spell out? This rule is for you and your friends own good. Drink and drive if ya so determined your not happy with how life is, I guarantee this will be one of your biggest regrets and you will be less happy with your new life.

How ya getting home? Like where ya live do ya? Oh is it

miles from town? Drink drivings alright then! No honestly, go on, try why dont ya?

Me I was all left, because it was my right side that was injured, and all the relationships that meant anything to me, and my gratitude, and the rest of my life, and manoeuvring obstacles and in society. Think your accepted, don't cause issues because when your alone in all your splendid isolation, doing nowt but consolation, you might get a little bored. Ya social animal!

4- Emotions rule - experiments, self driving cars. ethics, emotions, disability acceptance.

Emotions rule: Machines are said not to be able to make decisions based on ethics, neither can humans in a hurry or emotional moment.

Ever hear about the samaritans rushing to the lecture hall? Experimenters placed a poorly dressed man in obvious discomfort on their path. How many ethics or morals are misplaced? How many good Samaritans rushed by? How many other religious or otherwise folk dispel their teaching in times of need? Apparent or not.

None of these good people stopped to offer help, that is not to say they are not good people, most people with an agender on their mind will defer what they live by to attain that agender.

Back to technology, the self driving car, will, I only think swerve into oncoming traffic rather than hit a child. This can be said to be ethical but I suspect the car would do this as opposed to hit any obstacle.

Ethics and morals play, or rather underplay a huge part in the lives of those socially hardened people with disabilities. Religious or not, men and women are sometimes inclined to turn the other cheek, just figure the percentage of the average citizen that defy expectation.

New rules are made after disability is introduced to much of society. Programmer or political bias can influence liberty in man and machine but would you rather be in the reactive car driven by a machine or a drunk teenager?

The emotions of the persons with a disability, are somewhat nulled somewhat heightened. We know from personal experience to ignore a lot of what goes on everyday even when accompanying onlookers say did you did not notice that did you, probably best. Or we can rise to extreme anger at the smallest injunction because they are so ridiculous and tedious that we have just had enough. Even this those of us will toughen up to but tempers can flare at seeming insignificances. Those with a mind intact and senses to enable will tolerate and show temperance and wit in their response or lack of, but as most of disability is assumed there are those not able to, maybe. I suspect in their own way, socially acceptable and warranted or not cope and deal with these situations in their own ways.

We think in groups, things, social aptitudes are developed in groups. No one person is responsible for the alienation of disability, this has em merged through centuries and only in the latter has disability acceptance gained ground.

Policies and movements are made in groups, there is a large group of people opposing the inbuilt regimes that people with impairments face but just as this has taken years to evolve this has taken generations to start change in other minds.

There is still the conflict of right and wrong in self-judgement, what I propose by this is that some people are inclined to do the right thing some the wrong thing not because they are choosing individuality but because they are caught up in group think. There are many pioneers who have this individuality choice presupposed and this is becoming prominent, my promising outlook infers.

I learn bits, I sense a lot but I have not studied many academic areas so take my writing how you will, as a personal memoir to learn by I am hoping. My writing style has evolved much so do not be surprised if you witness something you disagree with or is not entirely correct. My purpose is apparent, to decline drink/drug driving and to enhance disability equality and inclusion. I want to cause debate amongst all people and education is a priority.

5- establish sense - Avoidance.

Establish sense, even in your thought, misapprehended speech can result in detrimental consequence. All the things I suggest are the faults of my life, I have experience of all I talk about, I am not a professor but trust me I wish I did not but I do know. You can avoid this and lead a productive life when you listen to these.

A few people, professional or friend are against me because of my mistaken past. Know where you are going and what path you are on if you have not yet decided.

6- Facades deduce - Good intention, jealousy, false fronts, ignorance, childhood.

All the good intention I have and there is still jealousy and false fronts. They are never gonna keep me down! I ascertain victory over all obstacle trying to hinder such a good cause. My suggestion and speech has made this hindrance more apparent, do not think you cannot control your existence because this is one of the main learnings in life.

As a child you vulnerable, susceptible and at the mercy of

your caregivers but as you mature and once, however finally you appreciate this sentiment thus will a new life emerge.

Think that control of your environment is feasible because this is the truest statement, all speech, thought intention and ignorance will deliver. Rules wavered and diligence ignored will head you for difficulty even as you found life easy or not. The rewards will produce much more for you if you take the narrow difficult path, broad is the gate that many find and walk, easy is this way. Challenges and character building are hard to find, you may say that you would rather not have challenges in your way but this leads to a simple non-productive life and no character encapsulation.

If you would dare just ignore the teaching and regulations and find a truly obnoxious path to try and follow. I will be the first to admit, I know this very well because in part I did this resulting in catastrophic implication that is near impossible to navigate but not un explorable.

7- Follow your purpose - Differing forms of people.
follow your purpose, follow your heart no matter what. Things will grow good. Material objects can have meaning, they can matter but dont let this sway without reason. If no one believes in you but you've always had, just a feeling then believe in yourself and follow this feeling. People arrive in forms, form one are good advisors, honest truthful advisors, these are worth recognizing and listening to. Form two however are to be mistrusted they are either misled or devious, or possibly absolutely naive through no fault of their own. No matter who from you learn the treachery against you as one grows, am not talking down to

or degrading anyone just this is fact. As is the good deeds done to you, you will greatly regard these more.

No matter the teaching I was dealt I was one of those totally naive individuals who could not be swayed, because of my prowess or abilities I denied all except those abilities were outweighed by stubborn naivety and prowess was egotistical to little life knowledge actually. I knew what I enjoyed, how to make people laugh and my then current wants but I did not know the meaning of life or how to sustain a healthy world view and other vicissitudes.

Ignorance will lead to your own destruction, when I heard words akin to this I blissfully waned them off as mature people thinking they know my life better than I do, well possibly or possibly not your life but certainly overall existence. You want to exist? Then recognize all words and actions and single out those you adamantly listen to, you will decipher the wrong from the right.

Because I relied on my magnificent colourful imagination that I thought was a mind needing no input I veered off path, got into trouble including drugs, fights and drunk driving. I was to be taught by life nearly ending and forever changed then on. You want to really learn, learn now or carry on the path of self destruction and face having no choice but to acclimatize an all altered existence, or die.

Myself I find it hard to in the past imagine me saying all I say but I cannot believe how I have matured in my growing years and since a life changing incident.

As you learn of things that you dont regard, have no current meaning for you or seem by the wayside you will later recall these lessons, be this not too late. Catastrophe is what it has taken for me to finally alter my ways and really learn to be an adult, this has taken years and years of avoidable adjustments and living the consequences for what seems all my life.

I dream of training those who require to be taught and I will teach those who just havent had the chance or are self obsessed like I was or are too young to realise. You if honest quite possibly fit into one of these very broad categories or can honesty foretelling, realize another.

We can make a better place and this starts with each one of you. There was a beginning for me, all the obstacles on the journey I am still overcoming, life is the best medicine but also the biggest obstacle.

One can say dont let people divert you from your path, not always possible I say, people protect and defend and a mind in one of these modes can influence and just as easily be influenced. Your instinct can find your way back to the right path.

Learn and listen to yourself as well as good advice. Decline following the path of no moral or juvenile behaviour, any age group can do this even I am starting here.

I realize this all can be seen as common sense, but lives differ, abuse, suffering or other facets can dictate a moral upbringing. As I sense things the population still has a lot of issues that are helped with even uncommon common sense to really make this an in the majority topic.

Dont take offence just let all be taught to the immature and do your bit in evolution

8- Memories from my past - Is this really mental health?

The memories from my past are haunting, how can I continue with thoughts that are regarded as bad mental health to others. I have so much beneficial work to bring, perhaps yes I just need to be patient but this is hard, I am at my wits end, with occurrence justifying - All is made difficult, but I have acknowledged in the past and wrote that the difficulty on a path will lead to more satisfaction when overcome, this is therefore going to be one rewarding journey.

I have been as honest as my life allows, I am leaning towards more secrecy but my words have been blunt and to the point to have an impact. I am trying to deter catastrophes (drink driving and disability denials) but I learn through my writing and experience that I have much worth teaching others. Now I cannot be sure what world I live in but I know there are issues with families, society, self-esteem and that there are still drink drivers. This is enough to say that I should continue and the promised rewards intend I shall continue despite the knock backs and refusals, Whatever I am so eagerly awaiting will come to truth very soon I can feel.

I am not yet enlightened despite what people may or may not think, I am, I put down to my upbringing but I think there is something else involved. I am however extremely astute to emotions in others and bodily feeling/senses in myself. This can and will take me further but until then there are other influences and effectors that are near impossible to exempt from such a dull life. Don't get me wrong I enjoy my work, can sense others benefit but need proof. Either statistics or email or in some other fashion.

The super-natural, regarding my foundations has been taking form and to a lost mind is still hard to apprehend but people get used to anything and my familiarity is not justifying.

My writing is a lot from self knowledge but do I really know? I can express my thoughts when writing I will archive this in personal speech even holding myself when emotions rise. I once before mediation (again, is that even a word?), had these skills, I was as apt as many at articulating and expressing the smallest most difficult to verbalise statures. This is returning, and will definitely fill me with the upmost joy when it facilitates my wants for these causes.

Destination unknown but i just know that great things await me and my work.

I had life so easy and rewarding when was younger, I remember having the thought, it came true! That I would suffer as much as what I witnessed and not be so credited with a happy life, not to say I didn't have issues when young,I did. I was so empathetic that I seriously used to imagine living lives of the less fortunate existences I viewed.

You know what they say,imagination is the master key to all, be careful what you imagine, I am not worried though because I also distinctly imagined the miraculous which is yet to emerge fully

9- Mum- Brief my story.

My heightened awareness, in dubious areas leads to me actually realizing myself a bit more. I am still some of the time egotistical, do not know how or why because I really feel a failure in other places.

My writing demonstrates, to me anyway, irregular inconsistencies of which I am not proud of. In my last book I consoled Mum without explanation, I degraded her very much for which I expose this, Mum is and has been for years my very best friend, I cannot judge any parenting because I am not a parent.

We had multiple difficulties of which she dealt with astonishing efficiency, I however kept up stress levels in all of us and did not regard as much as I should have until recent years. You can say that that is all part of growing up but I am middle aged! A big trauma delayed this acknowledgement but also enhances this because of what she went through to remain by my side.

I have had masterful upheaval in the latter part of my life, average upheaval throughout my teens and so so stresses when young, ain't we all so what is so special about my life. The Mystical has built my entire life because I have purpose realised now.

| always had the thoughts and feelings that life was going to be good, I would do amazing things, the reason I am in debt is because I often thought I had found the answer, being multiple of them. What almost killed me was my saviour, the answer was there all along. If you find me hard to believe take a look at drinkdrivedeterrent mind travels amid purpose revealed by JD.R. You will never think in the same way about much.

I was slightly, ever so a bit much too honest, my publisher edited lots, I still propose truth but withhold the unessential. There are those that will get me and, I am hoping those that will not, just take this as unnecessary information.

I have started this my second book before the first is published and I am still not entirely sure what the main content will consist of.

Head-injury was just my thought, I have personal societal and familiar al experience of this resulting from drunk driving, take a look at my previous book if you want to forever determine yours or someone else appreciation. Drunk drive deterrent Mind travels amid purpose revealed by JD.R

I start from the very first time I drank and drove. I know very well that memory is affected by brain-damage but I can recall the thoughts I had and the feeling of making it home, oh this ain't so bad I can do this again. I was petrified at first, driving at way under the speed limit then I thought I had better speed up because I might look suspicious. Then before I knew it I was driving at excessive speeds the alcohol soon forgets first cautions.

My so called friends, I did not have many or long established ones, used to tell me to slow down, not one of them although they were in my car said you shouldn't drink drive its stupid. Not wanting to face their own vulnerability at getting in the car and don't think because I was speeding was the main reason I crashed, there was something in the road, this could happen to anyone.

I really don't know what a different mess I would be if I caused the passenger a head-injury resulting in disability and years of recovery.

That gives me another suggestion that was partly covered in my other book, I want to promote disability acceptance and inclusion so will no doubt talk about this, this is a work in progress but Divinity has got me this far so hold out for the best.

I sit here in all my seclusion desperately wanting to assist the world and I can I will if you are looking or listening at this. Where was I? Drunk-driving in the early days, if you have a minor skid or bump take this as a sign. I had many and never did take what was trying so hard to tell me, do not assume though you will not crash and potentially cripple yourself or kill your girlfriend or boyfriend on the very first drunken excursion.

I was even stopped by police after drinking earlier in the

day and breathalysed, I was just under the limit, he says from what you have told us and your reading you are very lucky, this does not happen often, take it a sign. Less than a month later I was in a-coma due to drunk driving!

I have a promised purpose, this is to help you all to not difficult sense, I saw the adverts, although I am pleased to say they are much more hard hitting now and I viewed the posters. We need something else, I used to give talks on these subjects and know, very proudly that I have stopped teenagers to hardened drink drivers from practising this absolute ridicule. If you want to check my story, disability is very easily apprehended, perhaps your mates won't even be around for that! I will stop any from being so naive.

Drink driving KILLS, is not a fanciful slogan this is more than the truth, if not physically this will kill your personality, your emotions, your entire livelihood, work, family and other relations the lot.

As a skint uneducated teen I was chuffed at saving twenty quid on a taxi home, now I would gladly have paid the last of my money as opposed to the twenty years since attempting to drive drunk.

Early days.

I cannot remember a thing of intensive care, what others tell me I did some embarrassing things, too embarrassing to mention. I woke in an animated place, did not think my Mum was really who she said and thought I was being witty outdoing all these sci-fi nurses and doctors. I was not outdoing them just another patient to them.

Disability.

You will have trouble getting in cars getting off and manoeuvring on buses or trains, walking saying you can still walk, on gravel or grass or ice or steps and uneven ground.

Brain-damage.

Full stop. You will have trouble with everything from getting on with those you love to filling our forms to being accepted the same from mates to getting even partly accepted by many in society as what you think you are still worth to accepting your own blasted denials

10- Psychology - Realities, beliefs, Zen.

this is a cause and effect reality, my misguided belief system is wrong. i dont fully believe in spirituality after all, not the kind i thought i knew, well dont agree with is a better way of saying. i believe only i make my reality.

perceived pleasure< or pain>

this is virtual reality, we act on perceptions and misperceptions, no difference between illusion and reality.

how do you create your world

this is such a great course i am two inches taller and significantly better looking.

thoughts and feelings are always interrelated, watch your thoughts match your feelings

the most misconstrued thought is outside causes feeling when it is my thought, i cause happiness or the opposite by my stream of thought

feelings are simple, drama is what creates the story, remove the story and the feelings are simple

we are sum of our history, 80% personality formed between 0-7yearsold, imprint period/ more like 80-95% values/beliefs are programmed. kids do not discriminate. they need good life advice.

dont read/look at or listen to crap.

born to succeed programmed to fail.

Depregramme yourself, programmes/values/beliefs,

money, family, honesty, hardwork, trust, honour/ego, nature of man, what you deserve,politics, religion, fairness, truth, success, respect.

zen, drill the truth, 99.97% isnt true

much of what we believe is in conflict

thoughts create feelings create actions

we are what we think, our thought creates our world

everything i am experiencing is a reflection of self, be the change you want to see the world, your view of the world changes when you change

believing something does not make true, believe something true but its illusion

99% of what we believe is not true. different levels of understanding leads to different reality

believe something, never check if true=dillusion

confirmation bias we block anything that doesnt support our belief system, dont let ego get in way, dont let lies lead way

find ultimate truth

reality therapy

3 illusions, we think we know other people, we think we know ourselves, we think we understand the world

-we know what other people tell us -we see through our biases -we often see what other people want us to, -we distort with our history, -we distort with our belief system -we distort with our self esteem, -miscommunication, - false associations

-we believe what other people tell us, we see through our biases, -we often see what others want us to, -we distort with our history, -we distort with our belief systems, we distort with our self esteem, -we cant see ourselves, - we hide/distort our pain

-"   " we makes serious logic errors, -we are a sample of one

ego a false sense of self created by unconscious identification with the mind.

proximity rule, avoidance can be beautiful.

rational emotive behavioural therapy.

sane be good to yourself, emotional, change behaviour, you dont have to be sick to get better

we think, we believe, action

a activating event, b belief, c consequence d dispute

disturbing event-feeling-action >yell >thought -self talk- rules >mad-bop

is the meaning you give the event

thought-feeling response always match. what am i feeling??

change stream of thought. like to think??

think? < mad (self talk) focus on belief

 how can i look at this in the positive. quality of input is quality of output

reduce negative self talk

belief systems, idea/story made up

have decided, with assistance, what i believe and what i create. i let go of past pain, guilt and regret. i learn from my past to make a better future in the now. contribution, getting the most out of life, do no harm. how can i contribute more.

remove old pain old suffering, false self, story, belief system, removal of illusions

struggle creates counter force, evey time someone pushes, pull when they pull push

you are not intelligent if, or gonna expand your awareness

when you are intoxicating yourself with cigarettes and alcohol, thats a form of denial

zen.

more open i am, more i receive,

each day like a student at their first class, i prepare my mind like a blank slate for the day to write upon.

three levels of understanding, i hear and i forget, i see and i remember, i do and i understand.

wisdom, taking everything in without filter, the philosophy of zen is about finding truth.

zen is about being completely alive, search for truth, de condition ourselves, enlightenment, serenity.

multiple levels of understanding, see the layer between things.

completely alive, connectedness, present, aware, blank slate, absorbing, enjoyment, contentment.

to lighten, no mind, let go of ego, be in now, seek wisdom within without, release.

search for truth, not mine not yours ultimate reality, useful, multiple truths, application.

how we recondition ourselves.

layers, layered truth, extra sensory awareness, new understanding.

live now, only time there is never trade now for later, past future illusion.

5 roots of suffering, not knowing whats real, grasping and clinging to the unreal, being afraid of the unreal and recoiling, identifying with imaginary self, fear of death.

all problems are maintained. the mind is a machine, designed to make meaning out of everything, the brain is a dumb goal seeking mechanism.

our responses are not a reaction to reality they are

preprogrammed responses to belief system... but thats just a story.

Identify strengthen, observe weaken ego.

Neurotic repetitive thought, stop, right lets go on to the solution.

Inside your mind you are the prisoner, jailer and hero. solve your own mental problem.

Learn to dis identify with mind. who covered your eye, why did ya keep this covered.

11- The mystical - Spirituality and deceit, because I thought.

spirituality is amazingly deceitful, i am either in a spiritual world or i am not, you cant effect me with your rules when you declined me. dont give me thought then blame me, dont scare me with other people and your mystical ways, make things good then make them bad and everyone thinks i am enlightened because of realising some things that i am given.

either enlighten me and keep out or fucking do one.

i have been told things my whole life, that were meaningless so i forgot them, by spiritually inclined people on the street, i am given all these statements, later than necessary to act on, as thought when they are messages from the divine. they come as thought because of my wrong programming of events. well if you are going to treat a human as spiritual you can allow for mistakes.

dont keep secrets from those you call spiritual, dont keeps secrets from yourself, you havent a clue of the entire story, i am never supposed to behave like this but you effected me so i do. i would rather you projected me back to my usual life upbringing and mine life and stayed away with your hopes of what you knew had a slim chance of occurring. remember i have been spoken incomprehensible words my whole life so i know someone knew, only God knows the truth and God will save me.

spiritual indeed, i cannot write a bigger misdemeanour.

spiritual people in the street, in the supermarket treat me funny because they 'know' they know better, well i am telling ya, they dont.

another thing, if spiritual people are going to have everyday commonly used words as their names dont be mistaken that they are being spoken about because these words arise in nearly every sentence, i thought a spiritual place was advanced, yeah i am human talking from human perspectives but dont try and half include any you seclude, prior programming errors or not. i only know, think i know, pretty sure i know because of these words spoken my whole life, that are reminded by divine message and the reaction i get. your world need a lot of sorting too before this can truly be regarded as superior.

i am telling ya, there is no such thing as wholly,truly spiritual, yes i am talking to each one of you who thinks or thinks they know they are spiritual. come from my existence then try to find an argument. deviousness and deceit are not spiritually describing words and that i have encountered all along this path.

Oh thoughts get listened to, do they so and acted on, well why not my actions considering that is what humans are taught, most of humanity anyway, except for those exceptionally lucky minority that had parenting in the know.

I was taught this does not matter what ya think, ya cannot control your thought, this all depends on what action ya take.

I do not mean to talk in slang but this is all enveloped from spiritual emphasis having influence.

Because they thought, they chose and because this was wrong my life suffers. Because they fear they have done wrong, they affect my thought, my life to detriments that expose. They take so I expose.

They did this to a fine brain then listened to all the thought produced by an inhibited brain, I no longer have a mind, you find our why in my other books, all I say here this was enabled by them.

My totally abstract thought came to light and now all people are the same, minus the minority lucky few billion who are my neighbours and soon to become friends. Ya have a human feeling sorry for the awakened, yeah residing in human only category of existence. Missing the true deed am I? You're missing the true picture of my time.

Why affect others to inform when just leads to paranoia, mistaken ordeals and the rest. Yeah so I did not complete every demand, what goes for me goes for every awakened person, why no? That said I am refused by yourselves, that is right not fully awakened so I am exempt from this consideration.

Why give me power beyond your control or at least choice, if ya knew how things would go? But oh, ya suddenly have choice when this goes how ya not like, well I do not like either and this was all instigated by yourselves!

Synchronicities are an outweighed area, what is the reason? Because my overwhelmed brain said so, well if I can own that power, you are taking nothing from me and I promote all and every productive word I ever spoke and thought. Think ya can break rules just because ya made them, what goes for one goes for all, I remake and write my own productions.

I make my life, my protection what I always knew this would be. I am the god of my life, me not mistaken thought or impeded upheaval.

12- Still have a brain - Lost my mind in rehab!

Break a bad habit, I have many I wish to subdue, noted today that the method I only started less than a week ago really works. I had enough of easy daily nourishment. So I visualized myself in the vicinity of acquiring this and rehearsed denying that, refusing this when offered, I succeeded quite easily and bought something of more nutritional value.

Start with this story because I want to emphasize how routine ingrained norms in the brain are easily navigated. Dont get me wrong I have much to work on but am trying even the un recommended or less popular avenues of overbearing these.

but there is a lot more to life than just accepting or battling with your mind. spiritual laws, how can laws govern the uninitiated, the misled, the tricked or misguided for responsible or not reason?

rehabilitation centres are full of trickery, this is a description; it is their jobs to trick clients into recovery. this works, this worked for me but because i was nearly a chosen for one big mission and my future endeavour was foreseen by the awakened, i was fooled in allsorts of angles and totally disregarded.

jealousy has haunted my time, i without much explanation will just say, a top neuro psychologist may have been jealous of an injured clients mind. he practised defence against psychic exploitation, i often saw him with gaping jaw at intricacies i know werent part of the schedule. i was that much in tune, astute, empathetic and humorous, i was proud of myself even before my rebirth at rehab! since my mind was taken and other effecting significant powers, i have had very muddled thought, loss of confidence and lack of belief in myself, so i searched and searched and i am locating possible ways out.

my childhood made me extremely emotionally sensitive outwardly, i am still astute, the small things are sensed, others think i am mind reading, i am not. i missed my chance at awakening once, i follow a similar path to my prior destiny in doing my best as a mere human to achieve mastery i never comprehended i was on the path to.

mere human influenced by spiritual forces, things i eat, thing i drink, think, physically do, thing i say and write. ok so some of these if they were fully regarded soon enough, can be rewarding but what i physically do prevents awareness until an episode has near past some of the time. the stuff i eat and drink effects my thought, i am told to stop eating! STOP f**king eating, if you are going to raise a mere child without added lessons or knowing, like the Buddha had, then ya cannot suppose he will ignore his inbuilt childhood lessons, ya need to eat! dont try and tell me for the first time a quarter way through my life, potentially, to stop eating.

though i have bent these laws to suit my now limited existence, what i say productively goes that way, i have repaired the past, my thoughts and all, made my future magnificent and a shining light effective and changed my destiny, after all, absolutely anything is possible in spiritual realms. so my life is not what this was designed as but will remain just as effecting and enhancing and enjoyable.

i have struggled, against friends, family, my own mind, whats left of this but i still witness the end of the tunnel. family have given up on me,professionals dont always know whats best, except those that know. one of them, she is a social worker called lisa, now she is a hero. you might not be aware of the lingo i use yet, hero/enemy from someone helping you home to someone bumping into ya, and every facet in between, above and below, these i learned to regard as either hero or enemy, i dont intend superman or war, just figure of speech.

so ya never do know the path that will unfold, less thou are born awakened, as some are. a path of treachery can lead to a life of bliss and vice versa. i am going to utilise what i have learned for my anti drunk drive message.

ya think you have done wrong, ya have regrets, then you are given a mission. you dont adhere to all the faculties so treachery, turned bliss changes back to treachery. thought this was difficult when ya did not have a clue did ya? crawl out this hole ya appear to reside in, then watch people making all the mistakes you made without saying anything or trying to warn them. good luck.

13- Summer - Crazy days, early awareness in hospital.

The summer was great, days fishing, playing football or in the local pub until late. I passed my driving test that summer, this was after lonely relocation, had couple of good mates later on but used to spend a lot of time with early teens, I was 18, they were just boys.

This is the story of a regarded as unfair, difficult life leading to lack of regard which eventually effected the rest of my life.

What a present, for my birthday my Grandparents paid for

a motor, finally I could get more independence. It was a warm night, I had two very young adolescents in my car. An average looking 1litre Metro, I was proud of this but it was tediously slow even with pedal to the metal.

It was a dark night, we pulled up down a back lane for a crafty joint.

On the way back out I was seeing double, didn't adjust my driving, in fact I was belting along, in my tediously slow 1litre, round the corner except I didn't make this bend, I crashed into the bushes sliding up an embankment.

So stoned We weren't phased, got out made some adjustments to the knackered undercarriage of my car and went zooming off again. If the tree was closer and bushes did not slow us this would have been catastrophic I am in no doubt.

Very late to mature I was acting younger than these two boys.

In another town, I was on my own, we had moved to the country, my life was very quiet I was often out by myself with nothing to do no where to go. I would park right under the cameras and head for a solemn drink in a pub or club.

Drank shots back then, I would come to my car legless and no questions ask, I was driving home, cannot afford a taxi, Â£20 was more than my life was worth!

Pelting in a thirty limit I misjudged the bend again. There was quite a drop to the path beneath.

The only thing stopping me from smashing down into a lowered walkway was a metal guardrail, dented this very badly, mounted the curb and punctured a tyre.

I was reckless indeed but refused to take heed of what these incidents were telling me. In fact a fresh recollection,

I had taken heed in as much as I was not speeding on this road. The near misses had scared me I was slowing down to beneath the speed limit but I was still drunk, you will crash at any speed don't think because you are going within the limit that you are safe.

You might not think you drive recklessly but equally the double vision from whatever the intoxicant and two feet to the side and you are head on with that tree or you miss the railing and plunge ten feet into the shopfront.

Take all warnings, minor and major as somebody watching over you and granting a second, third, fourth, fiftieth chance!

They say those caught drunk driving have practised this something like sixty times before arrest or are you caught out? No matter how adept you think you are at handling the road you can be caught out on you one hundredth drunken excursion, and crash and kill and die. If you live good chances are one life has died and you are starting surrealism from here because you will not be the same person, will not think the same, walk the same if at all, talk the same or relate in your old way.

I had a new job in a new town, fresh start you might say, but no. We had been playing pool drinking all afternoon in the pub where all my new friends lived.

I lived down a dual carriageway, went onto this and immediately there was flashing lights behind me, I slowed to let them past but they stayed behind, eventually I pulled over.

The policeman said you were a bit all over as you came onto the main road,have you been drinking?

Oh no this was it, I really done it now, job, friends and social life all gone, though I did not appreciate this at the time, I calmly said yes but that was hours ago, I told a fib as to how much I had drank, he proceeded to breathalyse me.

First beep recognises alcohol on your breath second beep is the decider that your over the limit.

So I had no qualms when came the initial beep but waited for the longest few seconds of my life, it never made another sound.

Wow your just under, I can tell you've had more than you say, this doesn't happen often, take this as a sign. Relieved but not truly acknowledged, my move to the country would have been over without my car.

Blazaay I drove home.

Less than a month later we were going clubbing, remember laughing with all my mates.

Today I used to go to the club by myself and sit pitiful watching the dance floor.

Anyway we came outside all merry, got in the car...

Then I woke in a dream, science fiction had taken over, people acting like doctors and nurses think I cannot suss out that the matrix is taken over and nothing or no one is real.

Whats the deal they reckon I was drunk driving but I had stopped that foolish game, I can remember slowing right down.

My friends were now all in wheelchairs or bedridden, I used to choke at dinner time, so called nurses come into the toilet and wipe my ass for me. Surreal ain't the phrase , surrealism times infinity!

I was content making patterns on the ceiling with my gaze then an angel walked in! NO, NO, NO.

This is really happening. I used to work with her.

I still did not catch on, I told her the abstract truth, that Mum wasn't really who she said, all these people think they are fooling me, I have had enough of this film I want to go home. Was out last night can remember conversation.

It had been three months in intensive care, in a-coma.

Then I said I am going to escape and call my real Mum, she will not believe this.

Skidded, hit the curb, put my head through the window, take out parked cars and a brick wall.

This was enough, fate had had enough of me not listening, this was serious.

What if we'd gone in the river and drowned? My mate accompanied me with cuts and bruises in the ambulance, he had to watch me lose consciousness. The signs were not good

14- Susan - Unintended judgements, companionship, judgement, a death.

Unintended judgements are very apparent and most are susceptible to this. Example; did you see the looks on the judges faces when Susan Boyle walked out on Britains Got Talent? She had not even said anything and there were disgusting looks of immediate denials. This is a totally different scenario but alike occurrence to Disability except this lady probably did not get these looks in all situations, every street she walked up and every encounter she made.

I get that she was not the usual attendee but book, cover, don't comes to mind again. I guess the same can be assumed if an overweight footballer walked on the pitch but I once knew a particularly stocky lad who could sprint as fast and have a very strong kick about.

Companionship; even acquainting possible friends is difficult for Disabled people, they each have their own assumptions and some are hard let go of no matter the proof or will be wrongly reinforced.

We cannot, I know even I believe in acquainting twin soul mates who you just feel a connection with but we all of us should not judge on first even second or third appearance. Judgements should be held back I believe until you can say, oh I am not going to say but this is a prolonged time if ever, certainly relationships years in the making.

Knew of one girl who always demonstrated self-control when this choosing a partner showed and though she had some self-esteem issues was very deliberate when she came to giving of herself emotionally and physically. I think life got on top of her though as she met one man later in life, who turned out to be a cunning and devious man, he had judged her where he wanted her to be and she placed wrongful judgement on him to embody the correct choice for a life partner and they were married within two months of acquainting. Needless to say this led to miserable expensive times for her when she put on weight, was living unhealthily and back then looked to have added years to her age. I am pleased to say within the same timescale of acquaintance to marriage the divorce proved a best move, now she looks twenty years younger, lost much weight and has started to smile again

Disability, whether unintended or not, devious or innocent is judged. I have been judged because of how I used to talk, walk, think and behave but I as many do, have proven Disability does not have to be ever enduring and will affect different people differently at various stages of life. I consider their may be exceptions in some cases for those unlucky ones but I think all this problem of judgement stems from categorizing and catastrophist any subjects you like. In her case, Susans judgements were made by age and appearance of usual participants. Disability is enough despite age or looks we have a lot to prove. Look at Steven Hawking, one of the most intelligent persons, I strongly suspect that people on acquainting even him would maybe talk down to him or in a sympathetic condescending tone.

So truthfully, even I know not the real reason for a majority of behaviour, so comprehend why psychologists and other experts who have studied Disability and societal effects are having troubles imposing a resolve.

I am doing my bit in a community of people that have fathoms to teach.

My bit includes the anti-drunk drive message, if you recoil or utterly do not like the sounds of what we all talk of then don't invite this into personal experience by dangerous driving, drink or drugs or perhaps you think yourself individual and immortal, or that you take things so careful you will make it home. I thought all these things at one stage, let me tell all, if you drink or drug drive destiny is not under your control, I don't have to prove anymore than the honest words I choose, if you refuse advice then you are playing the waiting game. Either law and money and freedom will affect or health and life will. Do you want to die that badly? A night out with mates or on a date is not worth the rest of your life!

You can feel free, do what you like, I did! All the advice and adverts I ignored Really recommend you do not drunk/drug drive or accept a lift in a drink/drug drivers vehicle. Me I would have rather walked home or slept on the path than be a passenger in my car but I had someone who used to get a lift with me after every night out, even at me denying their pleas to stop they still got in the vehicle, thank goodness none of them was so badly hurt as I was.

My old self died, not physically but this has taken decades to renew to not yet fully satisfactory levels. Who wants to follow this path, I can safely say no-one and that you're a fool in denial, as I was if you tempt chance. Chances are you will receive your own judgement and have to build a personality and character again. Am not apologizing for my harsh words, I talk from experience, in my talks people need to hear the truth for changes to be made. I have seen change occur in hardened offenders in the one hour presentation, what bewilders me is why all these specialists have not caught on to the blunt truth will redeem, I have seen this.

15- The door is wide - A new inception of disability exclusion and inclusion.

Recall having the thought the door is wide open to those with a new inception of disability exclusion and inclusion. Disability is as individual as we all are and stories although many overlap are to be as singular as the differences in people, everyone has a version of their own discrimination and acceptance, all can make a difference.

The more that give their version and join the movement surely the better equip the whole is to realise appreciate and accept.

Ones mortality faced is I think a strong influencer in affecting relationships between the impaired to the non-disabled, again self preservation is such an all bearing effector to disability integration with society. Most people don't like reminding of how delicate our bodies are, how easily a change to health can massively affect everyday living.

There are specialists who study disability and all associated impositions but personal stories and examples and display, I say from personal experience carry more power to be listened to the the most trained expert. There is something about an audience having more their senses used when learning to make capture of a message more enduring.

I have displayed this and silenced a fidgety hall of students with visual, auditory, emotional, sentimental and personal self-denial factors. The more feeling you can enhance in others the more will be listened to and kept a hold of, people don't have a choice when it comes to differing their ways, the other massive influencer in people is self-preservation, if they don't make the conscious choice they will uncontrollably unconsciously alter their ways and thinking to bring survival inline with what their whole being has witnessed.

Drunk driving and disability go hand in hand with approaches to getting a message heard and also, although I don't want to use disability this is an excellent deferral to drunk drive. All I have said about getting the audience to feel something, as many emotions as possible is made a definite direct fact when self-preservation is made by stories of thinking it was all easy but can lead just as easily to disabilities.

16- Intention; - A best society

This book is just part of my efforts for a best society, herein shall discriminate against notable causes. Societal attitudes toward drink driving and disability prejudices.

This will help promote equal treatment and defer drinkers from driving. I have done this myself only after tragic accident survivor became my label do I confuse as to why these messages are so hard to en grain.

I deliver the truth, with upmost honesty, do not care how I may appear to others I have a message or two.

Granted most of society disdain from drink driving and a good majority are not discriminators, but the vast minority and even those good intended at times, due to misinterpreted needs, are still doing both these offences.

I have made hardened offenders cry at realizing what they were tempting so this is why I am sure, you go through all my work and you will never disregard self or others again and if you consider yourself a non-disregarding person this will help toward proper appreciation and consideration.

My life seemed to come to an end although I am determined this is just the beginning of reparation for all.

I have enemies and heroes accompanying me I have spoken about these in my book Drunk drive deterrent, mind travels amid purpose revealed. The words I have utilized at various stages meant these and my work have been faced with mighty barriers, but I will not allow to example as a waste of time, this work has too much prominence.

17- Dont die a fool. The lessons are long and difficult or sudden and devastating.

Ones mortality faced is I think a strong influencer in affecting relationships between the impaired to the non-disabled, again self preservation is such an all bearing affector to disability integration with society. Most people don't like reminding of how delicate our bodies are, how easily a change to health can massively affect everyday living.

There are specialists who study disability and all associated impositions but personal stories and examples and display, I say from personal experience carry more power to be listened to the the most trained expert. There something about an audience having more their senses used when learning to make capture of a message more enduring.

I have displayed this and silenced a fidgety hall of students with visual, auditory, emotional, sentimental and personal self denial factors. The more feeling you can enhance in others the more will be listened to and kept a hold of, people don't have a choice when it comes to differing their ways, the other massive influencer in people is self-preservation, if they don't make the conscious choice they will uncontrollably unconsciously alter their ways and thinking to bring survival inline with what their whole being has witnessed.

Drunk driving and disability go hand in hand with approaches to getting a message heard and also, although I don't want to use disability this is an excellent deferral to drunk drive. All I have said about getting the audience to feel something, as many emotions as possible is made a definite direct fact when self preservation is made use of by stories of thinking it was all easy but can lead just as easy to disabilities

18- An abrupt close

An apt abrupt close, drink/drug-driving/speeding or any form of dangerous driving will have lasting consequences, quite often an abrupt end of something!

I am a lucky one, yet I know what you are thinking. Want my place?

You are thinking not likely, so you know the answers to that, never, ever think you are invincible or play with lives cos I am sure I dont need to tell ya any more, you will have regrets that equal your biggest mistakes.

Live long in prosperity, dont die a fool.

Mirror-Neurons.

Discovered in 1992 by Dr. Rizzolatti Are not as was first thought just active in the motor cortex, since this discovery the motor cortex in the brain is not considered merely the producer of movements but is suspected to affect cognitive functions such as space coding, motor learning, action understanding, and imitation.

Visual properties and observed actions are layman terms for theses Neurons. They can also take action to things that you hear.

The match between an observed motor act and its internal representation allows one to understand the goal of that movement.

At this point the recruiting of the neuronal substrate behind the organization of an intention action allows one to have a predictive representation of another's intended movement in a similar situation.

The context to the exact observed action is important, I was in a behind closed doors time of vital importance and I felt I needed to please this man with my responses. Whether or not a situation is feasible/accessible and if social rank is not objected to all allow facilitation. The fact I found this accessible shows what confidence I had in my mind's abilities.

I have had personal evidence of something else regarding Mirror Neurons, I did not know what or why, something causing me to copy acts I observed. Even traits I always found disgusting! I was becoming someone else; I did not know who or how, I had to find out.

I will tell of some totally out of character actions now.

Disability is more personally affecting than the visible difficulties, a deduction in confidence enhances brain to have overpowering control over my chosen functions, I was unknowingly in survival mode because of what I put up with every day from an understanding society.

Thing I found identifiable to desperate people attached to and needing to be liked, to be honest I found needy and a bit pathetic. They would offer someone they have just met things that you would give to a best friend, even reluctance here, or even things you would not give to them or even family even your Mum!

I explained this with a need to be liked and obviously itâ€™s hard for us to make friends. It is very hard but you will get there I did, at least for a bit but my experience is still offering me evidence, I started making friends (I only have one of the original left and sometimes I even consider him less but just today he offered me advice that I was glad to take).

He has changed much, I have known him for 8 years, before you say anything I do try to regard rightly but we have been through much, some silly behaviour.

I have been utterly used me in the past I will not forget this fact.

I am still waiting to ever being totally connected with someone, this is honestly me. I wonâ€™t trust many, because of my times I wonâ€™t trust any at least at first for a long time they have a lot to prove.

This might seem like I expect, I think I am guilty I expect from others what I donâ€™t/canâ€™t practice myself. I have tried to demonstrate how head-injury will affect and I have been reborn, before the turning point anyway. I quite expect you to be unsure of me I was unsure around people that behaved like I do sometimes, I have said I would not put up with me if I were others. I am lucky to have some understanding people who visit. I have better explained how a brain-injured survivor with so called mental health problems, with prior structural dissociation and mystical encounters may act. You may act similar when your past unhinged programming made things seem the opposite to agreeing with your trying to live a quiet everyday life. - to put it very mildly.

Motor learning and imitation.

The things I felt sorry for when people displayed, I started recognising when I did the exact same! I imitated what I observed in disabled people when young, offering someone Iâ€™d just met a great gift right down to facial expressions. The biggest most effecting thing was how my mind vanished.

I wonâ€™t go into detail I will just say a powerful man was given permission to take my mind, I thought this an impossibility my whole life, I first heard the story when I was about 15.

He with exaggeration shook his whole body after some hypnotic talking no doubt.

A few days later he prepped me with more hypnotics, gave me the trigger word and I uncontrollably mirrored the same. This was so uncomfortable and involuntary. I forgot everything he advised the few days before and thought thatâ€™s my life over, I canâ€™t live with an empty mind.

I threw myself out a house window the next day after deeply slicing my arms and wrists four times, then when in a free access hospital, I did a massive ridiculously big overdose, no wonder I was sick. Still planned to end my misery when admitted to the psychiatric ward. I grabbed the fire extinguisher and sat contemplating throwing it through a window then jumping out. It would have just bounced from the reinforced glass anyway.

In the next town when finally released from hospital, I was getting used to my new vague mind but lost my cares, I drank petrol n all sorts.

I have written this entire series with nothing but a void in my mind! This displays at times I am sure, but I want to emphasize that all my experiences mentioned had one catalyst and that was having a few too many drinks that night twenty years ago!

Cannot describe the feeling I had when I discovered Mirror Neurons, I thought I was going to get my mind back, there was a reason and Iâ€™d found it. I was relieved to have justified my involution.

I would love to get an EEG or an MEG scan of my brain, the things it would or wouldnâ€™t show will amaze, not even 0.001% of people have experienced what I have and I still consider I have, for a blank mind, an amazing brain.

What behavioural functions can mirror-like neurons in brains and minds subserve and what should we even consider the proper functions for which they have evolved?

An answer to this question pertains to their role for enabling, or facilitating certain kinds of social interactions such as imitation, simulation, perspective taking, empathy, compassion, and so forth.

recent research that suggests that mirroring â€" the process of activating oneâ€™ s own action control system while observing someone else acting â€" may be linked to the development of action understanding.

âŒ We think that by protecting ourselves from suffering we are being kind to ourselves. The truth is, we only become more fearful, more hardened, and more alienated. We experience ourselves as being separate from the whole. This separateness becomes like a prison for us, a prison that restricts us to our personal hopes and fears and to caring only for the people nearest to us. Curiously enough, if we primarily try to shield ourselves from discomfort, we suffer. Yet when we dont close off and we let our hearts break, we discover our kinship with all beings. (Pema Chodren, 2008)

Healing the fragmented selves of trauma survivors â€" Janina Fisher
New Frontiers in Mirror Neurons Research - Pier Francesco Ferrari, Giacomo Rizzolatti.
What goes for me...
This is maybe the most controversial piece I have written, but hear me out I am defending my sometimes-obvious attitudes. Well, it takes two to tango, wrong doing toward me even stretches to the Divine. How am I going to react? Briefly the setting...
I was in a totally different city, 'following my thoughts', on the main street I walked all the way up, turned round then back n forth, it's what I did till I received what to do. With success in other areas, I should add if you are not that way inclined feel free to think that's why I am under mental health.
I did this for an hour or two stopping at the pub every few

cycles. I was caught on camera, the police turned up and explained we've had reports of a vulnerable looking lad limping back n forth, what ya doing? Then they said where ya going? where do ya want to go? As if they were assisting me. We got in the police car, I lived far away so they weren't taking me home, I could not decide when they came out with an excuse to take me to the police station. Reluctantly I agreed, then..

They locked me in a cell, kept me waiting for ages and when they returned took me to a room to finger print me. I was no angel when younger, they have my prints on record! I refused; I was not detained so put up an argument. To my astonishment they wanted a saliva sample as well, I refused and they said you can do this the easy way or the hard way, we'll put you on the floor and force a sample.

They had that elegant mystical charm I came to recognize from Divine territories in hospital.

I had the right to refuse both samples, I had done nothing wrong. they broke the law by tricking an already vulnerable man into agreement.

It was within my rights to decline! I did not recall until today.

So, as you can see even Spiritual break the rules, so facing this at a vast disadvantage anyway it's not really what you call humane to pull a stunt like this.

I cannot recall which police station or any name but this is not a problem I have with an officer just like I no longer have an issue with the psychologist, I am going to the top, the Divine allowed this to cover themselves, I am a mere human and they went to all this trouble.

Well, that becomes artillery if they carry on injustices and malpractice. Man, they think they can tell where I'm going to be and what I am thinking at any time of the day, only if theyâ€™re very smart. So why the false trickery from almighty power, talk about David and Goliath!

You see where my lack of regard comes from now, I hope. I am changing the world, I said in my writing that we should all be ok to talk Spiritual and that I am going to lead the way. This will happen in the future but I think this revelation of evolution is beyond time to show.

I always knew I would potentially be responsible for Spiritual evolution of this planet. Cannot believe I forgot this, it demonstrates the power I once had, and powers that I can hold on to, I am publishing a book (this book), this book will save resources, be used in schools or colleges and universities and other establishments even issued by the courts to offenders all over the globe.

Ignorance started from not appreciating just my own mind and its abilities. This added to not finding work that I was content in doing, which is one reason for carrying over into isolation and drinking for consolidation of what I considered a hard life- just appreciate those who have things worse than you but still get on with life. This then carried over into fighting and disrespect which all effects mind, the sub-conscious takes notes of all and will determine your outlook, you thinking and self-talk and believe me or not, take what you will, goes onto effect your physical body and health. Which goes on to be re-recorded by the sub-conscious. All this effects your conscious mind. You can think yourself successful by thinking success equally you can think yourself healthy by thinking of health and having healthy thought only.

Started driving, do I need to tell you what the drinker did?
. .
Crashed my car. Five months hospital not including the following years and years of rehabilitation and mental-health units.

Language of your mind
What you think may be just as harmful as that you do physically, so repair all them bad thought you had, now. All you need do is readjust them in your thinking repeatedly and soon enough you will acknowledge structures, whatever they were, redeeming in your surrounding or maybe they are in your mind. All I talk of has been tried and tested by myself and believe I did not enter voluntarily, I found myself in a destitute place so I researched my pants off and dug myself out of that hole, still climbing but I am a climber.

Have no bad thought about another or an argument or situation of conflict, this can only add to the bad feeling, you will think good of the worst situation, you think good of your enemies and before you know they are your friends.

Only think about truth, it is true that you can accomplish absolutely, absolutely anything with your mind. Only good thought shall enter and remain, negative thought is replaced instantly with pro-active good feeling thought. Go on, test my hypothesis, do this repeatedly enough and you reap the benefit even if they seem different to the original thought, thou must learn the language of the mind which is different to the language of the sub-conscious mind, which you must also learn.

The most successful, richest, prudent people know all this, why do you think they got to where they get?

Hope you are driving your life, how do you go on the road? Do you ever tempt fate? That one time could be enough. Speeding, drinking/drug driving or are you just plain reckless? You can be as careful as you assume, no-one can stop what is going to happen if you keep this going. Drink/drug driving, speeding will catch you out in the end. Hope no-one is, well if anyone is hurt is only fair this will be the irresponsible driver.

Introduction.

You can become an expert in any area when you view occurrences from multiple angles, not just these but the tangible too, personal relations, deeds, emotive qualities and other unseen traits and facets of life.

What just my aura and words without you maybe even realising teaches; anti-drunk-driving, why we do not get this yet I do know, because the lessons are taught all wrong. Every one lives with survival instincts determining their ways and a massive, hidden to a lot instincts practised unconsciously is self-preservation.

Make it visual (hobble back n forth), make it audible (shout really loudly), and potentially take something dear away something personal (it is so easily done, you too can end up walking like me or worse, in a wheelchair.)

Pass the feeling silence the room.

Every aspect of my personality and how I process my deeds and work are a lesson in themselves.

Have deliberately left this work with the odd abstract

linguistics to portray the damaging past.

My damaging past is obvious when you meet me, well not so much as it was if I were just sat in a room you wouldnâ€™t know but get familiar with me and this is obvious! The magnitudes that my only two, (one Â½ mate now) put up with, I wouldnâ€™t do the same if the shoes were reversed! Many mates have come and gone, short-lived for this very reason.

I am privileged and certainly did not ever think this would happen. See my dreams are coming true and there is no magnitude to the height of the dream. Talk more on this later, all I will say here is keep your dreams and ambition colossal.

If you fail tell others

I make use of all attributes that I fail at to educate the one of the biggest lessons of my time, drunk driving. Do this if you so wish to end up like me, I walk and talk differently, I even write differently, I think differently, was much worse before I was reborn. Not no issue no more.

The people around me, friends, there arenâ€™t many, I can count them on two fingers, and yes one might be the index finger and the one next to it! ...and that is aimed at the remaining two, they do me no good. They are big drinkers who use venomous speech and only one of them very occasionally says something that causes me to actually have a thought.

As I was saying the people who know me have all learned by me just by being in contact, they see what I go through and what I write and hear what I say, I can say that most of the people I have ever acquainted since the accident would not ever drink-drive.

This book I firmly believe is an excellent present to those you love, no matter their ages, or for your school, college or university or work colleagues. Mates, perhaps you probably know drink-drivers, perhaps you are educating your or another’s child or children or even adults. If they can appreciate the sentiment behind a gift they shall remain eternally grateful.

I will stop any one who crosses my path from drink and drug driving!

Want a cure to drink-driving? This will work. My history involves drink-driving and my ongoing future is deterring drink-driving.

Personal stories of disability and society and realities will affect you more than laws.

There are many memoirs to come but do not be fooled, this is not a conceited self-fulfilment so I thought we would start early with the potential results of living these memoirs. You can acquaint such qualified attributes and life skills.

Every trip out was filled with horrors that society found acceptable. I hobbled to the traffic lights two girls started laughing loudly at how I seemed, oh well they were young. Then a teenager passed me but came rushing back, brushed passed me just to press the button on the crossing lights for me. I carried on,

Further along on the same journey, a woman coming toward me looked up saw me shook her head and crossed a busy road instead of pass me on the pavement. I carried on.

I was in town with mum, went to the voluntary bureau, the woman looked at me daft, I hobbled over after nearly falling over, asked her a question and unbelievably she swung her chair round and shouted the answer to my question at mum who was stood near the entrance. I carried on.

Nearly fell down the escalator in the foyer, five minutes later I was exiting, I was one hundred meters away from the doors, a woman looking back saw me coming and fully opened the door and held it wide open for me. I know she was trying to be nice but these acts are insulting to disabled people. Fair enough hold a door if the person is about to come through but waiting for a whole minute just says â€˜I find you incapable,â€™ I got in I can get out. I carried on.

Just outside the very same door I tripped and stumbled a little, a man saw this and came over with a glutton look on his face, he asked me for a cigarette, I said no, he then gave me a sob story why he urgently needed money for the train, I said no, he asked for something else, I carried on.

Can you not imagine every trip out including all this and other detrimental behaviour? This behaviour you might find acceptable, perhaps you even do this, well I am telling you to stop. If the person is in a wheelchair or is obviously going to have trouble then you can wait as long as your life allows! But otherwise, I really recommend you stop this behaviour, donâ€™t become less courteous but do treat people equally.

Your subconscious will listen as you say thanks to the boy for helping with the button or the woman helping with the door and think you must want this treatment so it changes you internally and externally, fact, it is science.

Well-meaning well-wishers unknowingly harm you as much as scroungers or ignorance, I really hope I am educating, you will know if you are being wrong or if help is really needed.

Can you not put yourself in such a situation? Disability prejudice has many faces but a lot think that they are being nice.
A wealth of experiences taken simply as hard and unfair at the time led to a life full of important lessons later regarded much, so my work seemly is part memoir that is because there are things to be learned from my whole life story, wish I was taught exactly what life has shown me so feel obliged to teach these very lessons you can learn much from devastation. Do you wish for this in your own lives or will you learn from my life?
Always wanted to educate others in important lessons but underestimated myself, my life has shown me I know some vital things if you want to succeed and even live an ordinarily productive life. By ordinary I intend to teach something magnificent but maybe you are happy with just simply a plain productive life with nothing from the ordinary, have knowledge that can transmute the ordinary to extra.

Thought a calm first 20 years of my life was to continue, unemployment, study, searching unsuccessfully in all the wrong places and few friends since school age, moved home the year I left school and my existence got quieter and quieter.
From driving in the wrong lane, to conquering a self he never knew.

Visual mind.

ever knew.

Childhood was an absolute fairy tale, climbed trees and collected insects, united the whole playground to a mass game of football and won every race on sports day. Lived with Mum and Sis, though he never realized it he missed having a Father figure to teach him vital lessons of growth. Learned all his life the hard way, I shall stop myself there.

Considering less fortunate people I have had an acceptable life, lives would not be lives if we did not all experience the good and the best. Am learning, will never utter a less than opposite.

This continued into adulthood but he thought these lessons were meant to get easier, instead came the hardest trial to date.

He had friends to share his time with, should regard these memories as life was to get lonely. He had an impeccably visual mind and an astonishing imagination, could visualize anything and he did, this made him feel with might his life was profound but he figured he was nothing special and we all could do this with our minds. Later years he would discover it was no coincidence. He was to adopt the value of visualizing for healing, it is more powerful than he inclined.

Did not so much require being as mediacracy suitably fitting as he was, his mind would keep him company and occupy him, from an early age he did not realise but his reality was largely in the mindâ€™s eye. He too was to unfold this truth more in decadeâ€™s time.

He has heard it best not to live in the past, does not have a wealth of memories anyway, he was so caught up in his colourful mind that most of life slipped by without notice, he just remembers the poor events so its best he does not transport back.

Imagination can and will take you anywhere, the mind does not distinguish between a real event and a pure imagined one.

There is little I can teach about being a child, except to the elders, he wishes with his shoulders that he was encouraged more to appreciation of hidden emotive, invisible qualities, independence and other foundations of adulthood and given more responsibilities. Serious conversation was replaced with little belief and expectation, he figures he would be more today if more was expected from even the kid in him. After all what a kid learns stays with them, if they learn little that stays with them, treat a kid like a child and they will meld into your desire. He did not have social parents this effects the childâ€™s growth as well.

A want to express has always laid, as a fairly non-expressive character he has though got some knowledge to share, wisdom has grown in his years, something bound after treachery. He faced a challenge and after so promising a start in life he began by not comprehending, he was certain of his destiny, how did this appear but it was not to be the worst.

He is an adult now having badly sown seeds he reaped the harvest, but eventually he recalls the Diamond seeds heâ€™d sown long ago and continues by making these prominent in thought, in mind so they will effect change.

Mind travels, Purpose uncovered.

He floated through the first part of his time oblivious to life determining dogma, he really struggled when he required wisdom but this was growing in him.

Badly sown seeds probably caused the reason to commit to searching for answers, it also led to him having to really concentrate on who he was and what he was about and this leads to purpose unveiling. He became the architect of his identity as he was unfortunately identified by Disability after never growing up rightful, he immaturely severely injured himself.

He had a drunk-driving car crash when 21, the entry and introduction into adulthood was mangled! Because of his limited learning and other tremendously effecting, character warping incidents or baggage this was an extra test on his durability.

He met with obstacles like heâ€™d never witnessed, the crash became obsolete and not the most determining. He learned appreciation and finally regarded his mind, he did not put to use its agility until devastation inferred, use it or lose it, and he lost it! This is how he learned to appreciate, he went on a self-made mission and discovered that a vibrant mind is helpful but certainly not necessary for a happy, productive and creative life.

On he goes alongside essences and advantages, solitude and stigma, he turns all his quiet time into writing and recording. His life will not be worthless helping him develop into a life educator. He began talks on Disability and anti-drunk-driving, carefully using the previous as his tool to defer, this was very successful. He once proclaimed defeat, and drank lots in consolidation but he found strength and rebuilt himself entirely through self-healing. He now wants to educate the world he so believes his work will enhance sense and wellbeing.

Diamond seeds

He along with vivid mind dreamt dreams that create worlds. He has a vision to alter the figures for drunk drive deaths and train the people in mind, powers we all own, reality, wellbeing and healing in people who drive with stupor or hold stigmas or lack belief or want to improve themselves and their surroundings, reality making is where he is at today. He is embarking on the biggest most rewarding and worthwhile mission. This with a lost mind. He did not comprehend to satisfy the need for reward when he was too adept at dreaming so it slapped him and landed on his lap, MAKE USE OF YOURSELF!

I always dreamed of having some benefit on the world but did not know how, this was meant to be, I cannot not change people in health promoting sense making life enhancing ways.

Life goes on, lost the plot at 21, no direction, drinking and drugs, fighting and driving, driving destiny and my car.

Had a colossal drunk-drive car crash.

Years of recovery, acceptance and denial, life finds us meeting, will not waste your time, virtually honour a life just because this life allows me to give you sublime teachings.

They taught me, still are so there is no reason you cannot make the best better and get this knowledge upfront.

I dream today of how life would have evolved if I knew this stuff punctually.

Began life.

Lacking substance, life skills education. Full of ignorance and a sort of self-importance. Was a dreamer but not dreams of goal ambition, success and love, just kid like daydreams.

Something kept telling me everything is going to be ok, this was the Divine talking, which I also did not regard, higher-power guiding my thought.

Feel like I am finding that path where things are good after travelling many journeys up many pathways. With many losses and continued opposition, I am strong enough to overcome this. Do not ever doubt yourself or believe in fanciful horror stories if you are told these.

I am adept at this advice for one main reason, you live through an experience and you can become proficient or even expert.

Lived life.

In disregard, little gratitude and no belief just kept asking with my mighty mind why am I so lucky to get all this, something has got to come of this, but I did not know what.

Failed to grow up in my prior reality, so was forced to in a beginning twisted one. Reached Divinity and through my words warped my reality again, then I had to rebuild my amazing path and continued with effort to reach the enlightening experiences of this sacred planet.

Careful how and what you speak, think and imagine, only do these in good ways that enable your best to emerge and it will.

Find myself here, drunk-driving nearly killed me but since given me the most rewarding experiences. Talking to large audiences as a person who considered himself a bit intimidated, making a definite difference in the attitudes of others for the best. Witnessing not only children learning but adults too, not only witnessing but creating that masterful learning environment for all.

I am trying to lead others in my success so they can produce the same and finally if not totally then in the majority eradicate dangerous drunk/drug-driving and promote disability equality. We can do this. All.

I have published this book, and am going to wait for income from this.

Then my ambition is to fund an educational comic on this topic, then I want to fund film making about my entire story. Cannot currently afford one tenth of this, I am getting loans, signing up to money making suggestions and yes wasting a bit!

I spend all my money on this aim, I have today taken a weeks worth of money down to the last Â£3, it seems no-one but me believes as I do, want to get this book going, will sacrifice all I have to do it! No-one else had a vast impact on drink drivers, I will! Even if in a generation time, future youth will not even think, this will be inbred and habitual, an instinct not to even contemplate this killer.

Any who can support my work with any suggestions please get in touch and it will materialize quicker, otherwise I am hard done by and could take ages. Like I say, my life involves not much else but thinking and acting on this cause, I so wish to dedicate my lifetime to.

Realisations always known but taken for granted

Am starting from where I am at today, it has been a mighty journey but I am starting to realize and think better, at least try my best.

Am often talking about my life long ago when I present

knowledge of what is waiting at the edge of drunk driving. Making aware helps people from ever tempting to drink-drive.

Can help you sustain and not ever do this by drawing all your attention with a few words, when you do not want these in your own experience you remember all I say.

Drunk-driving is a direct path leading to either loss of identity because of injury. Lack of acceptance because of debilitation after injury, criminal records or fines, prison because of effecting other lives or to the extreme end of life/lives. The first couple mentioned which I have knowledge of can seem this an equal.

If you dare to drunk-drive or get in the car when the drivers had a drink, are you tempting fate? Course you are, do you not believe? In chance? In probability?

Many miracles brought me to today, did not believe in the correct things so was shown the way.

I am changing peopleâ€™s attitude for the benefit of everyone.

Plan to connect with other recoveries of all natures, we all have unforeseen stories of realities less known so have lessons to impart before a need to acquire the experience. Will you join me there or will you prevent deterioration even death of lives, relative or not?

Have done much work, writing and talks in the early days, have learnt as much since. Used to scare people from drunk-driving with horror stories BOf sorts of what you can expect in one realm. Am approaching this different, want to speak more of the miraculous, serene life. I have witnessed many vistas and ensure a regard is always held so dangerous past-times and neglect of anything or anyone is going not to infer.

Powers are available to us all, what do you think about? How do you compose your thoughts and speech? This has gotten me into a pickle, because I did not regard the magnitude of simple imagination or harsh thinking, so the choice was taken from me.

Try to think and speak in kind proactive words, and never utter a bad thing about others or yourself. I can offer good advice because I did not follow this advice, what do they say? Follow your own advice, this is often the best you will get but myself I am good at advice sharing but not so good at advice listening no matter who this comes by and so I know of the consequences, just like driving dangerous I have knowledge, you quickly become an expert when seen a situation from multiple sides.

Do you dream, do you day dream? Dream big nothing puts a limit on the magnitude of desires. Be careful though what you imagine, this is the factor in creation of your reality.

Had me some negative visualizations they started coming true. Did my best when I learned the true nature of thought and counteracted these bad thoughts with dreaming and imagining and writing the sublime instead.

These proactive thoughts are more difficult it is easier for us all to dwell on the negative but the best thought has chance of materializing too.

My life is and always has been designed by my mind ...with some colossal inferences but my childish colourful vivid imagination has evolved so far from the terrible to the supreme and back again.

Learned because I did a lot wrong but I go on and

encourage the best, this is what I should have done all the time, do not be near get this right from the start and serenity is yours. I think this is never too late to subdue your own mind, though I have made the winding path more difficult I will gain more when I traverse.

We all take differing routes but the staple is the same for each, think best, act best, believe best and achieve best.

May you all have the best you can.

Man has control over creation

Were you aware? Does that change anything for you? Let it begin a new wave of viewing and thinking about your surroundings, after all you are the master of your time. Cannot stress this enough, have written and intend to talk about the understanding of the powers you with your mind possess. It is no secret to those who search knowledge but little comprehended by most. I can take you out of your current dilemmas and seeming fixed detriments, whatever they may or may not be and take you up the shiny staircase into the light of no conformity and fresh new agendas.

Convincing yourself of your desired reality involves holding the conception of that, which must be defined by feeling. Feeling is the secret, assume the feeling and capture it for successful manifestations are felt, feeling a state produces that state. Desires encased by feeling are creative tools. This is the art of realizing your dreams. Put in to practice your Divine right wisely through your ability to think and feel you have dominion over all creation. Use your conception of the ideal self as the drop-off being the seed you sow, this seed will germinate and grow believe and you shall receive, sensation precedes manifestation. Feel the wish fulfilled in the present. Feel how you feel because your wish is realized. Call desire into being and yield to an already accomplished wish. This is vital, consider it done, not a future will be but a present, is, event. Imagine and always expecting the best outcome, really have expectation your wish is arriving. Passive expectation sums up what you will be feeling. Faith is feeling, have faith in receiving. As a man is, so does he see, to him that hath more shall be given, to him that hath not, it shall be taken away.

Never did regard your mindful ability much, certainly did not put it to use in any fashion except toxic pleasures, use it or lose it, and you lose.
It may be taken away, great purpose was to line up and promise of magnificence on its return, but the wrong roads were trod. Deeds of only thought disgust but ghostly stand. You have a teaching masterful in disguise but question releasing it.

Poem just written explain my difficulty.

Obedient moral
Activity overlay sensory
Beep siren replenish
Mine thought satisfies not me
Current enough even quiet
Induce pristine dream imagined ago

Gist win recline swill
Say winding path end shall compete
Messages from Heaven
Myself written not know when
Inspire right transmit plight
And show direct.

Challenge.
Authenticity obstructed constructed
Amid issues she is at the market
Intensify expect magnificence
Brilliance redemption alliances form
Succession possession

Ahead of hour know deed
Abundances are creed
Manifest no jest
Create dreamt fate
Believe retrieve

Concentration no temptation
Supremacy fates
Are calendar dates
Connect legacy no fallacy
Wild mild cognition
Truth desire became ignition

Fallow but strength

Rise from demise
Triumph is near
Long winding path trod
Found God

Serenity in the city
Mighty mission undone
Implanted agendas
Infinity unifies
New goals accompany
Battle seems but victory beams
Rite like sleep, true to keep, own misplace, shall find grace.
Maps of meant enchant benchmark, reach and teach.
Thankya

Had a moment, that's allowed. Nothing shall defeat, am challenged repeatedly but light shines and speaks to me at the right moment inspiring me to keep going, find strength, I am strong I am love shall accomplish my desire.

Not giving in, am obliged to repair. I undo every negative thought, and switch to thinking of only proactive acts of bliss and kindness, was challenged from the past but that is past now that cannot affect me anymore.

SOCIETAL RESTORATION

Received an email it said sorry we cannot promote your business.

WHAT! It's not a business, I make no money, though would like to turn this into my career and income. I never asked to be promoted for my own sake. It's a societal uplift and restoration, a worldwide catastrophic epidemic I am promoting a repair for, needs sharing so the messages are heard. This is a social business,

I would welcome support of any kind, look on for an inspiration.

Rightly or wrongly, it was my mind, mine!

I will talk about wrong doing.

I was in rehab for just over a year, it cost thousands I was lucky enough to have it paid for. The psychologist knew from day one what he would do and that I was close but not the chosen, still he dragged it out, put me off and easily obliged to no psychiatric input. He was making money the centre was making money by me being there, public money paid for this privilege.

I was reborn into a better than ever state but all the psychological tussling of mind meant I was still vulnerable and needed to ease back into society and daily living. Instead, he and/or Divine powers thought it a good move, because I might, maybe but probably not, (nearly his exact words), go on to a great important path, of teaching and educating the anti-drink-drive message.

They knew the whole time I fail to qualify, make disgusting errors and make a sham out of a gem of an opportunity. They also knew that if I do not make it, which I probably will not there is a second man coming along, he is the chosen and he will make it.

Anyway, he goes on with a power of magnitude to take my mind! It will be returned if I make it. Then send me on a literally mindless mission to see if I am good enough.

Please make your mind up and find some morals about other lives and recovery and public money and valuable time. This has been a pattern for drink drivers entering rehab for years. I met an unlucky soul when I was 16 who proclaimed he had had his mind taken, â€˜I think you will too, don't go to rehab.â€™ Is what he told.

This was over 20 years ago and the shrink told me we have been told only go ahead if you think they are the chosen. Well, I know spiritually enlightened people are aware of more than to go about and mistakenly take someone's mind that is their own. Fair so it happened to me, I was second in line and still have great things set before me but this has been going on for over twenty years. People go, people trust, people are shattered under false pretence and lies! Where is the respect in that from a moral upstanding role model figure of authority? Where are the Divine regards? I thought God is Love. Ah I am getting emotional, thatâ€™s all I have to say, I am not sorry for breaking your rules, they do not fit my model of reality, nor do some of the characters that have your backing. I create, I create, I create, I create, I create, I create, I create my existence, my fortune, my luck and my destiny, and itâ€™s far from your ideas. I achieve massive goals, I change bad habits in myself and society, I unite my dreams and no obstacle stop this, I dissolve any and all things in my way.

Have been debating whether to and how to get that out, I think I mention it later but did not have clarity in writing it.

I put out a Telecosmogram the other day, it included more

connection and inspiration and guidance, also inspire my writing. The past two days are evidence its working!

A truth

THE TURNAROUND- I was 25 I had that tragic crash just before I was 22, I had proved the professionals wrong and gathered myself enough to live and look after myself on my own. I lived in a small city, I used to hobble around it every day, kids used to laugh, adults used to divert over the road but I was determined I was going to get better. I had a massive disability and was knocked out of my mind.

I was deemed not to be coping, I was doing fine and I had an amazing lady friend we used to laugh so much. She was patient she would have to wait for the punchline, but we managed and laughed so.

From over a long stretch of time strangers in the street would approach me and give me a riddle I did not comprehend, when I was 19 someone told me do not go to Rehab, you have a car crash do not go to Rehab, if you do don't stay until the end. I said if I need to go then course I will. I was bewildered. There were numerous other unfathomable words said to me by a number of people over the years, I don't remember all of them, then in my 19th year despite being told not to work at a certain theme park I got a job there. I had fun I was 19 going on 15, I used to get in a fight every time we went to town on a night out, but I was protected because little didnâ€™t I know it I had a very important purpose ahead of me.

We were amongst the staff chalets another day on the balcony, people were mingling, a group came to pass me this lad got chatting, to my astonishment he said kill ya-self before your 21!

I took offence, what, what do ya mean, why? No, no way, I would never kill myself. He calmly replied you will regret it. I was bewildered, I walked of sombre and contemplative, what did my future hold?

I had a connective thought when I was 16 that everything will be okay. I eventually left work and had to move back home.

Back to 25 years old, I would walk we would laugh, I would walk some more. Going to Rehabilitation was suggested to me, What I can get better mentally and physically? There was no question, I was going, I had forgotten all the parables I had been told, I went. My lady friend did not think I should go, she had the same demeanour as all these riddler's. If you get in a fight just exit, she said, half-way through the year I did get in a tussle with some lad who had a lot of issues. I went home for the weekend thinking I was going to quit but when I returned, he had been moved to a more secure unit, he had smashed a large internal window and they swiftly moved him on. I was relieved and thoughts of going soon faded, I was hopeful, I had made amazing improvements in all areas, so I felt I could get even better. I got selfish towards the end of a year-long stay, I had dumbfounded the psychologist with my cognitive recovery and made great improvements physically but I thought I feel absolutely amazing, better than ever, I wonder how far I can take it. I was reborn and I wanted more!

One day I was waiting in the consulting room for the psychologist and I was having a cigarette at the back door. He came in and I immediately said you have an amazing job! I felt supremely wonderful. I should add here I was also told back at the theme park exit Rehab when the psychologist has an amazing job. How will I know when that is? I questioned.

Did not recall this until after. I stayed and it happened a few days later, we were in session then he pronounced this is a Spiritual world. This sounds interesting I thought, he had my attention.

He went on to foretell my future. You are to be tested on a mission to check you're suitable, he carried on, he told me what I would encounter, what I should do and what I would probably do. All the experiences and people I would meet places I would go, what I should do and what I would probably end up doing. Some of it was so far-fetched I didn't believe him, that doesn't sound like me at all, I protested, he had also told me there were two of us going through rehab at different times, the chosen one could be either, so I was sure he had the wrong person. What I find sick about it all was that he laughed loudly giggling throughout when he received what I would probably do.

I went on to, without mind I must say face obscenities and opposition and spooky experience. The future I was told will not get a word in, I am a strong believer in creating your own destiny and possibilities are endless. I rewrote the rulebook and cancelled much doubt. Largely assisted by masses of research.

He said how I would go on to teach and deter drink-driving, in schools, colleges and I was to do the Uni where I would experience profound connection. I would become a household name. He continued your mind is passed to me, I will iron out any issues then when youâ€™re on this mission go to the love-dragon go downstairs, (not actual name but colours and words came to have another meaning for me).

The obscenities mentioned, try not to think too much about this statement or it can become yours! Just try to picture a place where all your thoughts seem controlled outside of yourself and any, absolutely anything stimulating in whatever degree causes thoughts that you are uncomfortable with or even disagree with- This was influenced mental-health issue! That is how I later qualified as a sufferer, oh give in this is not mental it is mystical! I was put on an injection after other strong medication.

I will be there, at the dragon he said, shake my hand you will get your improved mind back, a copy of my mind and become enlightened. Sounds good I will make it I was so confident. I made it to outside the love dragon, I left my photographs on the bridge where I was meant to, the man put the umbrella down on the table further along pointing to where I was to put my suitcase, I left it right there then just stood highly confused, I did not know what to do I was in no healthy mind.

Back in rehab he did an extreme body shiver, two days later I uncontrollably mirrored it, I walked out silently thinking something terrible had just happened. I threw myself out a first-floor window the week after I was born again! Then I deeply sliced my arms and wrists, then took a massive overdose. I since discovered Mirror-Neurons in each of our brains, does exactly what it says on the tin, this explained much of my conforming to disability expectations that I found wrong my whole life, and I was adhering to. More in book2.

After this mission he predicted rightly that I would be put up by the council in a bed & breaky he told me stay in every day and read what I had written (my first book) and when I could go out, what pub to go in and what pub not to, the pub I should stay in the landlady was a dream, I liked her, I was told at a BSSK event by a tarot reader to go into the pantry and kiss her. I am not that forward but if I had we would probably still be together now.

Again, I did not recall this until after, of all the messages I received I wasn't sent one at crucial times when I was supposed to remember something. All these words from my past that I include are not remembered memories, they are influenced by thoughts that just appear as memories. I should have told myself, anything I need to know, I shall hear in a womanâ€™s voice, not my own thought. Can you judge how mixed I was having all these thought that I wasnâ€™t choosing? Any way I did not go through my book, went out and drank every night which was a no no and I did not kiss the landlady.

A council place had become available in a town I did not favour, you just watch it will be in such and such estate or the middle of town. I was given three choices two were on such and such estate, another was opposite a nightclub above a kebab shop, one was a street with a name that sent chills. I went for the best of the three, not like that was fixed or anything. A few days later I saw a board up against a top window it said B.S on it, usually I would say that stands for bull s**t but because of my recent dealings with the B.S.S.K I thought it stands for school.

Do not s**t in the school, was another riddle I remember. Did, do not drink in the school, I did, do not go in that shop, did. Do not walk there or here, did. When the fairs in town I was meant to do not exit town, just go and take nothing but bring what you need or something like that. I was so fed up, all the times I could have received a useful message I did not. Now I was trying to live a normal life, I get a barrage of reminders, like I am remembering all the riddles from over the years only they were not memories. Fed up I gave in and marched into town while the fair was on, went to three pubs I was told to stay out of, walked past all the caravans, I was not meant to, looked at people I was told to avoid and walked where I was told not to. I have read a little on psychology even I know put an idea in some oneâ€™s head and they will quite likely take that option, anyway I was in no fit mind to be on a mission of any kind.

The psychologist hung on till the last minute, I had a grant that paid a lot of money for me to attend rehab, I find it a bit backward, help promote my wellbeing then as I am reborn take all my mental capacities. I affected things because of this, I was working on empty and that text I sent was thought to be a want by my subconscious so it came to pass, I had a very muddled mind, I am ashamed of how I approached a truly Divine mission and the baggage I created others, but I have since repaired. Anything is possible!

Thing is people knew about my responses my whole life,

they tried to warn me but having what I considered a good memory in my ignorant youth actually meant I recalled nothing but a few things. So many effects of a fully known cause my life came to mean nothing and I mean I was blessed in mind, I find it difficult to comprehend why this was allowed to continue, as I was known not to be the chosen, information from the psychologist my Mum would just instinctively tell me when the second was going to rehab and I was to write to him with this along with lots of other information. I do not blame him, I did at first but I gain awareness of the significance of forgiveness, after all he was given permission to medal, what more do you need. Like I said it seemed backward but I would have never found this path if I remained my naÃ¯ve happy go lucky born-again ecstatic self. It has taken time and I am still in mourning but I keep occupied writing, I am quite familiar after the abstract, curvaceous, brilliantly entertaining mind of days gone to a pure empty and bland mind of today. Hey I know what resonates, can you not tell by this writing how articulate I must have been with mind working?

I was meant to exit town, just go but over-burdened I got a taxi to Mums, I did not know what else to do, she wasn't her usual self and she called the crisis team who came and took me to hospital where I was affected by Vu-Doo, (I know how to spell that but like colours words and letters mean differing category than youâ€™ll ever know), ghostly apparitions and more, spent the next year in various places a lost soul in Divine territories. Everyone was against me now until I was transferred to the city I used to live in, then the town I live in now. I hit rock bottom and was on lots of strong medication that I manage without today thanks to my self-healing and alcohol abstinence. (Latest, I have started drinking again and back on medication but I had bad times with one influenced tablet so I stopped that and am doing good.)

Do not think I am just a nutty professor, spiritual entanglement, do ya want some? Go on take my times.

My prophecy followed me for a while, I met up with men who just used me, the riddler's told me about. I felt powerless but I am making my own rules today. I learn my lessons well, my failures help me grow as a person, I succeed on my terms.

I became broad shouldered, I learned to forgive the psychologist, but when I lived in the town I did not favour I went to an outdoor shop and said do you sell hunting gear? What were you after? he replied, a shotgun I exclaimed, the looks were of horror I was obviously not in a state of mind to be let loose with a gun. I had the intention of going back to the Rehab centre, blasting the psychologist then turning the gun on myself, but it was never going to happen. I was so happy to be me as I grew, I had a wicked sense of humour and I was content with my looks albeit I had issues when younger and had a mean time living with a step-Parent. I have done my fair share of suffering I was bitter for a while but I forgive all those who have wronged me, I learn you do not need a picturesque vibrant mind to be happy, I can overcome defeat and rebuild myself internally to become the person I want to become, a better person that can forgive the seemingly unforgivable and move on putting it behind me to finally stop thinking about the experience and concentrate on what I can affect today, I got knocked down but I get up again, you are never going to keep me down. What is within my power? Ha what is out of reach is within my power, everything is in reach, everything!

Have lived the stuff of movies, I quote myself from my other writing I have had a fairly quiet existence, yeah with a multitude of sporadic colossal occurrences, I created apparently, I remember day dreaming about going into Rehab and making a miraculous recovery, be careful what you think about is the best advice I can give you.

Disability and my run in with a Neuro-Psychologist made me who I am today, I am not so ecstatically possessed with the quick visual mind that I used to be, I get more easily bored without my imagination up to scratch, I listened to my inner voice and found truly helpful audio-books, websites and rediscovered my passion for writing. I do not succeed at writing whatever pops in to my head so I am grateful to discover topics that energize me and are potentially helpful to others.

If there is a divine light or body of souls watching over, then why if I was able to receive messages of protection despite the fog of cigs and alcohol when I was younger, why on this... could I not receive at important moments when I was closer, given how important this is and how you tried so hard to get me here even though you knew all the time they reckon I fail. That is not a nice thing to do, oh I am sorry if you knew that then you would also predict all the work I still do and have done, okay so help me get this out there and witnessed by billions, show me, show everyone that you do regard lives, if there is a bigger cause then I have good to materialise. Here is the deal, if you want to call it such, let me view the figures of drink-drive accidents and fatalities drastically reducing and disability acceptance and regard dramatically increasing and you can regard my life as worth-while and nothing more, no pain no punishment, I did my best with what I was left with.

This is the story of my life, you learn from a blessed, hurtful, curious, plain, creative, struggle, teaching of a life.

#Beginning ORPHAN PHASE:
We are all similar to this flower, you and me, majestic and beautiful, but life or people have a nasty habit of ripping the petals off one at a time, slowly or suddenly then tearing us in half and throwing us in the gutter.
I can think of at least five times that immediately spring to mind, when I have been torn not only in half but into pieces!
My skin was the first to appear, I had Eczema but I was so young I accepted it without it affecting me. When I was at secondary school it was bad, peer pressure and all that, lost my self-esteem, hated being in front of people, disliked it when people invaded my space, couldnâ€™t face strangers without thinking I needed an explanation. When it was worse I used to lock myself in my bedroom, I wouldnâ€™t go out.
In my teens we had moved to a new town so I was extra uncomfortable trying to meet new friends, I didnâ€™t manage very well and I got a reputation as the one with the silent attitude, plus mystical awareness in some people meant they avoided me, more on mystics later.
My skin got worse, Iâ€™d had enough, I was miserable no-one understood what a barrier to face to face meetings

it was, I attempted to cry but was always incapable since a teen, I kept my emotions inside for reason two. So, one night at my wits end I took an overdose. Ha I half-heartedly swallowed five paracetamols! Do ya think that will be enough? Will that do it?

It was a cry for help, I told Mum the next day expecting some miracle manifestation as a result she calmly said that was silly wasnâ€™t it? Little did I know but my call for help was heard temporarily, when we moved to the next town, I got a live-in job, the uniform was a black T-shirt, oh great I thought. My Eczema cleared for the whole season. It no longer affected my interaction but I learned I still lacked confidence, the second having a large bearing on this.

Second equally, probably a bigger affecting thing, was a psychological torment who blew his rag at me, the seven-year-old, in the first week. This was the beginning of my emotional sensitivity, it developed over time with continued alertness required around the tormentor. I was so proud though of gaining this ability even though I did not know where it came from until much, much later. Yes proud, I could connect with people, emotionally I knew what they were feeling, was amazingly empathetic. Both qualities have been nulled because of the fourth and fifth subjects, mainly the fifth.

My bedroom was and always had been my place of solace. Torment innocent by his standards went on for years, I reached a teen and decided I would not put up with it any more, I think I said something prominent and stopped talking to him. Why I didnâ€™t grow up and move out I will never know, I should have stayed with my mates in my hometown.

Anyway, for years we never spoke a word, living in the same house pretending the other wasnâ€™t there. This made it difficult for others but people acclimatize to anything. I would live, eat, watch telly in my room only going downstairs to exit the building.

This time calved out my early disrespect and unease around some men. It affected how I communicated, when I relaxed, what I thought. It influenced a lot but the last two reasons had more impact than this feeble man.

Third influencer, we left my hometown, moved house the year I left school. All my best friends were gone, I have fond thoughts and memories of one in particular. We left a built-up area, went to a quieter plot then moved to the sticks, life got quieter and quieter, did not mingle or have a social-life until I started driving. The jobs were intensive or minimum wage, I did not enjoy any part of my life, life is not fair, I lost the plot. Started drinking and driving and began getting into bother and fighting. Was a wimp at school but my immediate response was life has toughened me up but I knew not that I had big purpose ahead and this mystical essence that affected every aspect was protecting me. My ego took over, I remained complacent though I just thought I wasnâ€™t easily intimidated, what rubbish! I never got in a fight with a man, they were drunk boys! I was just a drunk boy. With no desires no plans no ambition no life.

The fourth to appear was the biggest to date. Used to go clubbing every weekend, me and a mate were driving to the garage after the night out, I pelted round a corner and skidded, hit the curb, skidded back across the road, demolished two parked cars and took out a brick wall. He was okay, cuts and bruises, I lost consciousness in the ambulance. Unconscious for six weeks in a-coma one of them at one point from brain death.

Hospital: Mum is devoted, she was not gonna give up and my recovery is partly due to her insistences when I came round. I came-to on Christmas day but I was out of it, I donâ€™t remember any of A&E, I was in an early day's rehab centre for weeks before I had my first recall. I was bedridden sidebars up the bed. I was quite happy tracing lines on the ceiling. An angel walked in and her boyfriend, they were mates from a theme park I worked at, I lived with them. That is when this surrealism hit home as truth but still when I was able to move about in a wheelchair, I still thought look at them people thinking their Doctorâ€™s, why does everyone sound funny? Where's my real Mum, Iâ€™ll find a phone and call her, she will not believe this. My mind was scrambled but I could remember my phone number!

I went back to Mums to live, they warned me to rely on the chair, you what, I thought no way, I parked it up in the corner and never got back in.

Physio was delayed, I was administered a private physio from the social, I only made noticeable little improvements then hospital physio started.

Used to go to a day centre, we were all there, Social worker, Support staff, Mum and me, they said what are your hopes for the future? I replied that I wanted to move out, get my own place. I felt the energy in the room, they chuckled and thought that is not gonna happen for a long time, you cannot look after yourselfâ€¦ One year after release from hospital I was living on my own in my own place, this was one of the many disbelief point provers.

I struggled with my own company at first, I called Mum

lots but I had issues with her. She had to be patient and was always sounding sympathetic, this got to me. All else I did was walk, sorry hobble around the City, I thought the more walking I do the quicker I will get better, so I walked/hobbled/lurched for miles and miles every day.

I had to find something to vary my day, I joined another day centre, it wasnâ€™t really my cup but I was desperate. Soon I found and started voluntary work at a contact centre, you know where the Oldies gather and brew the kettle. I saw a look on the managerâ€™s face when I walked in, but I was cognitively slow back then I did not know what it meant. Then she would hassle me to get my mobile number for the coffee list. Coffee list why, no I never carry my mobile anyway.

I never added up the clues. She hassled me enough so I subdued one day and gave it to her, she immediately went out the door took a walk and text me, do not remember what she said but it was something likeâ€¦ I like you, we should get together. OH, THIS IS WHAT YOUR EXPRESSION MEANT! THIS MAKES ME REALLY HAPPY! Being disabled I did not chase women, I thought no one is gonna be interested in me. We went back to mine that night, I was over the moon, she visited often every night, and we laughed so much! She was understanding and patient with me, I would talk, get to the punchline, start laughing, stutter and stutter, she would have to wait for the humour. I have the fondest memory of this time; I did not comprehend then but years later I accept that I was in love.

Then it was suggested that I wasnâ€™t coping, you what?! I had a girlfriend (we never made it official but the sex was amazing, best ever, this suggested she was my girl), I laugh every day, I have a life! If you can call walking and laughing a life, but I was happy. I was managing ok, I cooked, did the housework, what are people looking at? I am managing fine.

I went to rehab, we never split up she did not think I should go, I kind of wish, I used to wish that I did not go but I am rebuilding, finding and planning the impossible. Determination is another big mind-altering drug. Anyway, I am in another city I meet the fifth imposer.

He spits his words, exclaims profanities in our first meeting, I was gonna dump the rehab idea but he justified his reasons so I stayed. I am gonna have to cut the story short. Am only on the fifth line of my mind map.

I want, I need to get all this completely saidâ€¦ It was a year after, I had made a profound, amazing recovery in every sense, the psychologist was proud of his work, I was amazed by his work, he performed a miracle. I was waiting for him, having a cig at the back door, he entered and looked at me enchanted. He could tell I had taken a leap forward; you have an amazing job! Is all I said, I felt better than ever in my life. They say anyone will benefit from rehab trauma or not, it is all about re-educating teaching to live to your best means.

A week after I was reborn, I was greedy, I should have left, I wanted to see how far I could take this glorious feeling. He settled, I was still buzzing not really in the moment, he divulged the start of something I did not like the sound ofâ€¦ Whether you believe me or not is not importantâ€¦ He explained what I would go on to do, something very important. The mystical was finally revealing. What I should do and what I would probably do. ..He ended by taking my mind! Story cut short. He gives me reason, I take, my naivety was confident, and then he sets a mission for future days.

Anyway, I failed that mission, miserably, I failed to regain my bettered mind, was adjusting to brokenness.

The weekend after I was reborn, I threw myself out a window, bounced off my bum. Cut my wrists, and stopped bleeding. Took a monumental overdose, threw it all up in the sink. I just could not injure myself! I was trying to end my life, I couldnâ€™t go on without my mind, my mind!

Back in hospitals for another six months. I could not handle facing the neighbours when I went home without my mind so I moved to start a new life. I used to put up a homeless bloke, well he kipped on a mattress in a brick shed, he wasnâ€™t gonna stay on my sofa, Iâ€™ve got lots of compact discâ€™s to guard. We would chat on our daily encounter, about life, about struggling and its effects, about philosophy.

He had such a happy outlook, all his suffering and his look on life was admirable. His thoughts and feelings later went on to determine his life. No-one, not even the social, would give him somewhere to live, but think good thoughts and luck will have your back. One landlord heard about him, and thought he has had enough bad luck, Iâ€™ll give him a chance and let him have a flat.

I moved home again because I had started voluntary work giving talks about drunk-driving, they were very successful, I heard many good things said. I was on telly, in the papers, on the radio. My confidence was higher than ever but I had a breakdown â€¦ of sorts, back in hospital, I am broken AGAIN! After the transfer and another six months I moved to a recommended town because I had lost my home and did not want to go back anyway.

I had lots of support, felt lost, briefly it went like this: lost in denial missing friends, accident, find happiness, go rehab one year, reborn, taken, broken, hospitals two times six months, lost, broken, near defeat, used, then a light, regain ambition, repair the impossible, aim for the impossible, partly regain my quality of mind, ditch the users, make big plans.

This was written a while back, keep getting mixed signs today. Think there is still a chance, yes there is, just do not knowâ€¦ no I do not think I am meant to go again.. or am I?

I donâ€™t think I have time to talk about the build-up in my current town, will just briefly skip over subjects I want to get on to the explorer stage, have had it with remaining in the past, even this writing is making me edgy.

Support changed, mystical that was backing me is now seeming against me, or was doing, drink and drugs, get used lots, felt vulnerable, get used some more, get evicted, move house, generally waste time, then a light, quit drinking and drugs go on my own mission: was doing great at the time of that writing, no more drugs but I like a drink still.

How did I react to the big life events: Repaired the angst between me and a certain man, finally, the accident didnâ€™t really give him a choice. Latest; Mystical effects us all, he proved he can be someone I can admire and get along with, today I cannot believe I even thought about giving him a yet another chance.

Itâ€™s what you display that comes from inside that matters.

We all have struggles, fond memories and lose friends, we

go on to discover a bigger world, start a new life and become a bit more cosmopolitan.

Mental health/brain-damage meant I did not consciously cope at all. I used what I had, did not live in the past, do not hold grudges.

Everyone has a story and the bigger ones will determine character building more. Plus, all the smaller milestones and turning points in between, this has been my life, these were my challenges.

Giving in AGAIN was a serious option but I chose to rise and deny defeat to make it here to inspire others, I still learn, I still grow. Do not ask too many questions because I am not sure on the facts but there was a light, I realized I could not carry-on self-destructing so I set and went on another mission, self-imposed for self-improvement, with a blank mind, how did I gain a belief it was even possible to make the best of what I had?

Not sure but early gains spurred me on.

Yes, sorry for skipping chunks, this is me practicing my presentation, I don't have time to detail every occurrence.
#Middle EXPLORER/WANDERER PHASE:
I dug, I uncovered, I delved and dabbled, Will not go into this much it is for you to discover but you really can enhance your life, outlook and beliefs by being the explorer. I dabbled in all of the following and experienced noticeable changes in my world: Tele-cosmic Power-mapping destiny your way. Genetics affecting biology by thought alone. Placebos- believe it and it materializes, your brain can convince your body to heal. Transcendental Meditation- a mindful meditation. Truths of reality- We and everything are pure energy all intimately connected.

How mind and thoughts create- Thoughts are things if you want it, dream it and expect it, it can be yours anything can. Self-discovery and Soul finding- You never knew that about yourself.

What are you challenged to do? What mission will you embark on? What discoveries can you make? How do they change you and your world, remember, change biology with thoughts, create reality with thought, create and determine an idealistic destiny.

How do you grow? Will you settle comfortably? Will you continue creating?

Or will you be defeated by the negativities you have made yourself?

A scientist did an experiment, this is fascinating, you will never look at anything in the same light nor will you disregard the slightest thing. He hooked a pot plant up to a polygraph, he was just contemplating, thinking what to do, I could burn a leaf to see if that does anything. He just had the thought nothing else, he never actually burnt anything, just had a thought, the polygraph went haywire! Wow. Next, he hooked up a pack of eggs, threw one in a pan of boiling water, the polygraph went mad, the other eggs were screaming! Wow, both sensed his thoughts and actions.

Disability: Just a few short stories because I am passionate about disability equality and imposition on people with disabilities.

-I was going to where I was a volunteer, I had to cross the road at the traffic lights. Just as I reached for the button to wait for the green man, I passed a teen. Suddenly he came running back, brushed past me and pressed the button for me! Then trotted off with a pleased look at being so meaningful in his community, he wasnâ€™t crossing. Gee I thought I could manage but my already socially conditioned persona and lack of ability to think of alternatives and the belief that disabled people just keep quiet and remain thankful, so I just said thanks.

-Further up the road near the railway level crossing I looked up, a woman was approaching, she saw my hobble, panicked, shook her head and immediately briskly crossed the road then carried on the same route there was nowhere else to go and no turning. Iâ€™ve seen this behaviour countless times, people would rather endanger themselves crossing a busy road than share the path and walk past the disabled person.

You may say they are just being considerate. What like them people who jump back ten feet and flap their arms handing over right of way? How considerate!

Please do not draw attention to me, I get plenty without doing anything abnormal but walking. The path is wide enough, I will not attack you, I will not kiss you, I am just as wary as you are the reactions I am waiting for.

-Another day I was in the mall, exiting about 100meters from the door, a woman exiting looked back as she was going through, walked back in, fully opened the door and waited holding it open. She waited for Iâ€™m guessing 30 seconds. This courtesy is often taken as an insult by disabled people.

Do not put yourself out for me I got in I can get out, is what I could have said but disabled people do not verbally attack any especially if they are trying to be nice.

This was just insulting but the timidity in me just said thanks.

-Then I exited walked round the corner, tripped and stumbled a bit, a passing lad hadâ€¦ I immediately identified it, a look of glee. Ha ha this is an opportunity, what can I blag out of him, what can I gain from him?

He came over and said you ainâ€™t got a cig have ya? No.
Then he gave a sob story why he needed money for the trainâ€¦ This is a common one, I have heard before, urgently needing public transport money. No.
He asked another favour, no because I knew what he was thinking before he did, I denied every request and carried on my eventful journey.
Please can you just imagine every trip to town being filled with vulgarities, people thinking they are being considerate but have no idea how they make themselves appear and just insult you then expect and probably get a thanks!
Or the simplicity of advantage takers. They have been prominent even after recovery but still with a vulnerable streak that opportunistâ€™s hone in on.
Alternatively, the innocent lovely people who just lack true understanding and patronize you with a petty voice, hello duck, nice day, come out often? Are you on your own? Who looks after you? What, you live on your own? Who cooks for you?
You bear it, tell them the complete truth and they assume poor boy he is deluded he thinks he manages on his own!
I am NOT picking! This is a massive invisible topic. It is how people are made and remade, even by a caring society.
My oh my, how do we go about treating this one, we have to start them young but teach the correct wanted

behaviour. People guilty of what I speak of are teaching their children to be wary, to patronize, to ignore, to sympathize or just let us pass. The latter probably being the most acceptable without flapping arms, stares at feet or jumping ten foot.

I people watch but there are so many rights and wrongs and differing opinions that some people for this reason are afraid even to make eye contact, unless they are heroes of any stature or enemies of the very small kind.

The subconscious, recorder of all, hears these behaviours, hears and records the thoughts induced thereof and affects change in biology, affecting the brain and the physical body.

I once heard, I was told from a wise source that disability, even physically, can be made worse by the ways it is dealt with! Yeah whatever maybe in your fairyland I first thought, but having been and seen and felt the changes, also I have witnessed the same thing said in different ways in books, I kid you not he spoke a truth!

Lecture over, go about your daily business just do not go against your will to do the right thing, do not feel you need to oblige because we are special,

you will know when you can specifically be helpful.

End WARRIOR PHASE:

Good beliefs to program:

You are on an adventure. You will be lost at times, broken at times and reborn at times. How you internally deal with these times will be the biggest deciding factor. Many think societies are the factor to watch, this is a hinging one but I would rather face society than an out-of-control mechanism in the brain/mind!

You start like an orphan, move on to explorer then become a warrior, meeting different scaled enemies (from the advantage taker to the psychologist) and heroes (from the lollipop lady to my so much missed laughing girlfriend, or nurses, Doctors, the psychologist can even fit this too, he helped me be reborn, I admire his skill and knowledge greatly).

Life is like a good story; these are the basic ingredients. They make you who you are, you can continue to make and develop to greatness.

Thinking about these talks, I adopted a belief that helps, is if I can do it once I can do it again. I had a breakdown of sorts, I thought I had lost the knack but I can do them again and I really consider they will be better, even with doing them the hard way. I will gain even more confidence!

If they can, I can. Look towards getting a role model who displays the qualities you want; it really helps to get inspired. I have been watching some talks and I have role models from other speakers.

Success is inevitable. Beliefs make or break.

How do you react to life? Your reactions determine your biology, which determines mind and body more so than the environment.

If I can, you can too. Believe Im no smarter than you, I have had part assistance but I did the research, I can make my luck, I can change the future,

I can create anything; I have developed my mind and body.

I feel stronger and more than I ever have.

Scripts from a lost mind
challenge
challenge
Authenticity obstructed constructed
Amid issues she is at the market
Intensify expect magnificence
Brilliance redemption alliances form
Succession possession

Ahead of hour know deed
Abundances are creed
Manifest no jest
Create dreamt fate
Believe retrieve

Concentration no temptation
Supremacy fates
Are calendar dates
Connect legacy no fallacy
Mild wild cognition
Truth desire became ignition
Fallow but strength
Rise from demise
Triumph is near
Long winding path trod
Found God
Serenity in the city
Mighty mission undone
Implanted agendas
Infinity unifies
New goals accompany

Battle seems but victory beams

Rite like sleep, true to keep, own misplace, shall find grace.

Maps of meant enchant benchmark, reach and teach.

Thankya

The mind emanated from the void, when the void became aware of itself.

The silent, no-mind is the void, aware of itself.

Walked through, do you want to delve? Enter!

Sometimes mystical and always life enhancing, not always apparent at the time, big lessons imparted herein started over 30 years ago.

Life is a big school, full of heroes and enemies that all will assist your growth. These lessons and the teachers are hard, but how much do you want to develop?

Have had trials and the downer years, didn't appreciate rightfully, was never ambitious, so life taught me lessons that at first destroyed me. Life also taught me that I have everything I required inside me already and to search, treasures abounded! Learned about myself and that it is more than feasible to reach golden new heights.

Developed my mind while recovering from severe Brain-Damage, discovered truths of reality, power of mind to create and heal and the nature of society plus much on the route.

Will take you to places you never have even regarded and heights you never knew possible even in your dreams.

Learn to look at yourself really and what you do, how you behave, how and what you think. Development, even those who do not feel the need will be shocked at the reality - bending impacts of self-discovery and improvement.

Began with lack of direction dropping out of school then college after college, the mighty school of life little I aware, was the teacher, teaching and the education was holistic for a certain life. Relocated much in my youth, while this affected me

It was not so apparent until adulthood. I learned at a young age unconsciously about facades and fronts that people including myself were putting on and how, wrongly so to oblige and fit into society. Family home life was challenging.

We briefly talk more later. My time has been filled with lows, a prominent influencer appeared near the beginning of these and stayed, this forced adjustment inbuilt some very emotive skill.

Was low in real grounding self-esteem and never had much in the way of girl-friends but used to get on better with feminine mates. The influencer's effect on me was wariness about adult males when young, that alongside my confidence being crushed because of another reason. Health and the environment were toughening me up, but way down this path we discover that neither have to to promote the most profound distilling change, that is our minds responsibility. Mind, how or what ways we react and think has a greater impact on well-being and health than the actual environment does! There was me thinking its a horrid society and the people are so difficult, this is not true!

Had I not seen enough troubles for a young life, obviously not because I had not seen even a blemish of the magnitude of difficulty I was to encounter. Lost the plot with health, family life, social life, forever relocating homes, unemployment, education decisions. Half-hearted attempts at suicide must have had some pronounced effect deep within my mind, would find out what it feels like to really attempt it in future years. After losing all sensibilities and becoming a drink-driver, fighting the world and its forces, which I was never going to win. Had an always on the cards car smash. Brain-Damage and Disability were my companions now, what an introduction to adulthood. Finally went for repair, this was a behind closed doors time of miracles, but another influencer influenced. Shortly after I was reborn, I lost my mind! Look on to be inspired, educated, trained and shocked. Surprised to realize life and yourselves.

This will be your beginning, a healing climb to new inner and outer scenarios.

This is a collection of scripts I put together into one, wrote them years ago, am not ashamed they show where I have come from.

Just one more

Grow accustomed to driving in peril

What limit
Leave go of a sacred life
Friends depart
Do you not respect your stance?
People stare
What will you do?
Life relapses
Do not regret the inevitable
Don't get in a car if the driver has been drinking
...And do not forget me
The news
I talk to God
This isnâ€™t the pinnacle
The demo
Life is no cure
How can you scare?
Legal obnoxious
Monsoon complexity
I surrender
I dread
Big Screens
Refractions between the light
On the ace
Screen, big screens
Digesting every pace
Rings of steel
My home does beckon
The voices, the metaphor
CCTV served till then
Transparent traffic on the door
Everywhere in everything
Itâ€™s starting in here

Shandi speakers do attempt
Rise with invention
Remember this
Clang for the big tables
With the lights out, redeem the famous
The dangerous
Slender outcome
Drown the woes
No job but to burden
Fleece a want and chalice
Search the hidden jewel
Upright until these feet can't stand
Barron are caves
Remedy the emptiness
Another pill to digest
Felt is the mission
Damned are the champions
My queen will visit
Mental wealth is calling
Why the heed
Sacrifice unto justice
A legislation is born
Saleability
Miss labels my price
Shallow fears
Walk on empty tears
Service re-pungent
Intolerable steam but meant
Insofar I stride
Come the crazy tide
Abyss yields a welcome place
Do I have something written on my face

Scaling eyes bright
Let us teach with lost might
Worthless battle the biggest surrender
Whose message is this sender
Hunger is burst
The first is always the worst
I am a statue
Eyes wide
Who's this in reckless abandon
Meet the subdued professionals
Sit in warm spaces
Nervousness keels aside
A mission is replanted
Months are the moths of distrust
Agility reconciles
Trauma mislaid
They knew I didn't
Twisted the morals of allowing
The time had come
Flee the scapegoat now
Stayed beyond the calling
Rose petal floors turn
The trickery is hidden
Born again
Killed again
Skewed
Your time costs my essence
and notes
A visit for treasure
and liqueur
Backwards you seem blunt are words
Your face is split

and back
Stabbing your intention
Just reading the words
I am here
Hold back on withdrawal
Fully aware of deed
Stitch up the balloon
Scandalous sleep on it
You owe me big
My decline
It became the worst in the world in my mind
The vagueness elapsed was never ending
An experience not common
I travelled through circles borne by the feelings of stillness
Feeling amid a sea of not knowing
Words free these feelings and I have none
Ignorance blemished fears encroached
Can anyone help
post rehab
The words are far
I reach out sincerely
To include a breadth of existence
My heart is the well
It should not be this way

Was always in to writing, did it partly as a hobby, not much though I was a talent at imaginative story telling at school for my English homework. Did not get into poetry much until I was a lot older. In fact the real poet in me only showed when I had a major personal topic that I felt deep connections to, the crash was revealing many hidden facets.

Following is a collection of poetry written in chunks years apart, I was very cognitively changeable and they are during different phases of my recovery over this time. So, display different thoughts, emotions and attitude. I do not think I have any since before the accident, have tried to roughly order them to sequence a story but the time of each is not accurate.

Ready for some stature revealing content, you may not find the will to continue after! Come on the journey, we will visit every level of my experience. I was freshly without mind at this time.

Found it so beneficial the overall feeling when I clumped all the previous poems into one, so have done the same here:

Treasure

Land on your feet and grace the view
Turn away
Run you will walk
Berries in the meadow
The material is compelling
Do you feel it
Deeds in the stone
Remember us
Beauty and the calling I feel
Rebel and the cause you seek
Sweet surrender begs
The coral and the ocean meet
Feel love in the light
Cover the epitomes

It is a roller-coaster of felt internal
Feel this warmth
Eternal aspirations
Rebirth
Let me live as a star in the sky
Shining for eternity
Fortune is stark
Rebirth
Let me live as a star in the sky
Shining for eternity
Fortune is stark
Wish a hospitable place was fate
Stop the toll before it is too late
Too late
Come back for me
The mist levels
Let me live evermore
Solace becomes the weak
Hopes are I never die
Thoughts lingual
This was already my debt
Into a dead niche
Memories of deceit
Association teams blood
tight close words
from here
Glorious
Beauty in time
Magnitude golden seconds
The comfort
Blush and reveal
Makes me feel, the amazement inside

Stamp your feet
I like how you brush your hair
I like how you know where to care
The way to bounce
The little snort when you giggle
Your aura propels
Your words capture
You are complete temptation
Utter â€¦ perfection
Understanding and patience
Belief and your dainty vigour
More of your truth is my goal
When two become one
You touch my sentiment
Embrace
Your way the mirror
I feel refined
Your appearance but holy
For me you fill the void utterly
Numbers but one
My years supply source
The rise of sun
The mere interlude
Centuries create equals
Beautiful days
Treasure forms in your shadow
Remedies the poison liqueur
Gratitude
Union before family royalty closer
Birth is nowt
How do you construct the deal?
Life

Let's live.

Regards, Misinterpreted Power, Trust, Loyalty, Love will remedy.

But my child is aDRINK-DRIVING EASILY DONE, HARD LIVED. But my child is a good person.

Learn the easy way! Live it before it is too late. Refuse drink-driving.

Or you can continue learning and readjusting to a ruptured existence.

What is your favoured learning style?? good person...